THE KINGS
KILBURN HIGH ROAD

BROTHERS OF THE BRUSH

Jimmy Murphy

THE KINGS OF THE KILBURN HIGH ROAD
and
BROTHERS OF THE BRUSH:
TWO PLAYS

OBERON BOOKS
LONDON

WWW.OBERONBOOKS.COM

First published in this collection in 2001 by Oberon Books Ltd
521 Caledonian Road, London N7 9RH
Tel: +44 (0) 20 7607 3637 / Fax: +44 (0) 20 7607 3629
e-mail: info@oberonbooks.com
www.oberonbooks.com

Brothers of the Brush first published by Oberon Books Ltd in 1995

A catalogue record for this book is available from the British
Library.

PB ISBN: 9781840021844

Cover design by James Illman

Contents

THE KINGS OF THE
KILBURN HIGH ROAD

In memory of Tommy Murphy
'*Fair thee well sweet Anna Liffey…*'

Characters

JAP KAVANAGH

MAURTEEN RODGERS

SHAY MULLIGAN

GIT MILLER

JOE MULLEN

All men are in their late forties

The Kings of the Kilburn High Road was first performed by Red Kettle Theatre Company at the Garter Lane Theatre, Waterford, on 12 June 2000, with the following cast:

JAP, Seán Lawlor

MAURTEEN, Eamon Hunt

SHAY, Joseph M Kelly

GIT, Noel O' Donovan

JOE, Frank O' Sullivan

Director, Jim Nolan

Designer, Ben Hennessy

Lighting Designer, Jim Daly

ACT ONE

Afternoon. The interior of a social club. An Irish crooner plays out from a jukebox. MAURTEEN RODGERS sits alone smoking, his elbows on his knees looking at the floor. JAP KAVANAGH, cigarette in mouth, is looking at himself in a wall mirror; straightening his tie, fixing his oiled hair back.

JAP: If there's one thing that can be said about yeh Jap Kavanagh, Yeh never lost it boy. Yeh never lost it!
    (*JAP combs his hair back as SHAY MULLIGAN Returns from the toilet zipping up his fly.*)
SHAY: Arra lads, lads! Who in the name of jaysus put that gobshite on! Daniel O Donnell, jays, if there's one thing I can't stand, it's that Donegal bastard.
JAP: He's not that bad Shay. All the women over here love him so they do.
SHAY: She has me driven mad with him at home. Mornin' noon an' night. D'yeh know what…d'yeh know feckin' what?, I even heard her call his name out in her sleep the other night.
    (*As JAP turns and winks at MAURTEEN.*)
JAP: Your Dierdre? Hah, thing's must be gettin' quare bad in the Mulligan household, what Maurteen!
SHAY: 'Daniel', she says, 'Daniel put your arms around me.'
JAP: D'yeh hear this Maurteen?
SHAY: 'Daniel you're so hot, you're so warm.'
JAP: And what did yeh do Shay, hah, hah?
SHAY: What did I do? I reached over, took up the glass of water with her false teeth in an' emptied it over her, false teeth an' all! Maybe that'll cool the two of yis down, says I, you an' Daniel. Yeh gummy bitch yeh.
    (*JAP laughs heartily. GIT MILLER returns with a tray of drinks. JAP rubs his hands in anticipation.*)
JAP: Now there's a sight!
GIT: Breakfast is Served!
SHAY: Good man Git.
    (*JAP clicks his heels together and salutes the tray of drinks.*)

JAP: Top of the morning, Mr Guinness, sir!

GIT: Do you know boys, I often wonder if there's a prettier sight than the first of the day?

JAP: Well if there is I've yet to see it.

(*GIT lifts the drinks off and sets them down.*)

GIT: Right, bitter for Shay, Jap, large bottle for you'n me an' Maurteen...

JAP: (*Cutting in, with a sting.*) Lemonade!

(*GIT holds it out to MAURTEEN as MAURTEEN gives JAP a look.*)

MAURTEEN: Lave it down there Git, thanks.

GIT: Got yeh the large bottle...it's cheaper that way.

MAURTEEN: Sound.

JAP: Did yeh not get him a straw aswell?

MAURTEEN: Jays, aren't yeh hilarious altogether?

JAP: What?

(*SHAY raises his glass.*)

SHAY: Well lads, for the day that's in it...slainté.

(*The others raise their glasses and mumble a reply.*)

ALL: Slainté mhaith.

(*A silence as they watch MAURTEEN pour his lemonade into a glass. He looks at them.*)

MAURTEEN: Somethin' wrong?

(*JAP shakes his head in disbelief.*)

JAP: Lemonade, jaysus, Mary an' Joseph. Lemonade, I ask yeh.

MAURTEEN: You'd swear it never passed your lips before.

JAP: You'll be pissin' all day with that Maurteen, pissin' all day, tell him Shay.

SHAY: Run the guts out 'a yeh that will.

MAURTEEN: Aren't they my guts?

JAP: God but yeh'd think yeh'd have a pint an' the day that's in it Maurteen.

MAURTEEN: For the last time Jap, I said I'm off the drink, okay?

JAP: And can't yeh give it up in the mornin'?

MAURTEEN: I'm off the drink alright? Been doin' too much of it lately, no harm cuttin' down.

JAP: Get up the yard!

MAURTEEN: What?

JAP: The fuckin' yard...get up it!

GIT: Hey, all the man's sayin' Jap is –

JAP: What? What's he sayin'; that he's a bit of a drink problem?

MAURTEEN: An' what if I have?

(*JAP laughs out.*)

JAP: D'yeh hear this fella?

MAURTEEN: What...?

JAP: 'What if I have?' Hah, that's a good one, that is.

SHAY: Look, if the man's saying he's off the drink then he's
off the drink, alright? It's no big deal.

JAP: Drink problem me arse!

MAURTEEN: Hey...!

JAP: Hey what? Ha, hey what?

(*A beat.*)

MAURTEEN: Just cut it out, alright?

JAP: You tryin' to say you're an alcoholic, hah, hah?

GIT: Ah come on, will you lave it out Jap?

JAP: Listen here fella, there's a mighty difference between a
heavy drinker an' an alcoholic.

MAURTEEN: That so?

JAP: Mighty difference.

GIT: Just lave it, Jap, will yah?

JAP: See Maurteen, you're just a heavy drinker, that's all.

MAURTEEN: God, but aren't you a very observant man
altogether now?

JAP: Mean I'm more of an alcoholic than yis all put together an'
there's not a bother on me...is there? Don't see me havin' to
give it up, hah?

MAURTEEN: (*Shouting.*) Could you ever just shut the fuck up
Jap, hah, just keep your fuckin' trap shut for wan minute!
(*A silence falls for a moment.*)

GIT: (*Sheepishly.*) Happy now? We'll end up gettin' fucked out
of here if this keeps up.

JAP: Jaysus sake man, all I'm sayin' is why'd yeh have to give
up the drink today of all days?

SHAY: Who gives a fuck, hah…hah? Who gives a fuck? Do you Git, no… I don't, so let it go Jap, okay?

(*JAP puts his hands up in surrender. A slight pause.*)

MAURTEEN: We're gettin' a new kitchen in okay? I'm knockin' the soup on the head till I've saved enough.

GIT: See?

(*GIT crosses and looks out the window again.*)

JAP: Savin'! Jaysus, can't yeh get a loan or somethin'?

MAURTEEN: I never borry nothin'. If I can't pay for it me-self, it don't come into the house.

GIT: Look, are we goin' to have to listen to this shite all mornin'?

JAP: Supposed to be a wake Git, fuckin' wake. Mean how yeh supposed to wake a man with lemonade, hah, tell me that? How yeh s'posed to pay your respect?

MAURTEEN: Pay me respects in me own way, okay?

JAP: Poor Jackie'll be turnin' in his grave.

MAURTEEN: Yeah, well lucky him.

JAP: Hey! Hey fuckin' hey now Maurteen.

MAURTEEN: What?

JAP: You tell me what.

MAURTEEN: Well…isn't it well for him?

JAP: Well for him? Well fuckin' for him? D'yeh hear this fella lads?

GIT: Hey, can yeh watch the fuckin' language Jap, fuck sake man. Bridie was good enough to let us have this room.

JAP: Just gone fifty an' he's in his grave, don't see how it's well for him, s'all I'm sayin'.

MAURTEEN: Isn't he well rid of this poxy town once an' for all?

JAP: Rid of it? And what's that supposed to mean?

MAURTEEN: Means he's the only one of us that managed to get the hell out of it an' back home.

JAP: Hey, hey! No one keepin' yeh here cowboy. Travel shop five minutes up the road. Paki that own it s'only too happy to take your pounds, shillin's an' pence off'a yeh.

MAURTEEN: That a fact now?

JAP: Fuckin' fact boy. And after you've bought your ticket there's a good book shop 'cross the road sellin' plenty of maps of the good ole Emerald Isle.

MAURTEEN: Don't need no maps, me.

JAP: Maps an' guide books, great selection, what lads?

MAURTEEN: Said don't need no maps, okay?

JAP: Hah!

MAURTEEN: You bein' cute?

JAP: Twelve years man! Twelve fuckin' years since yeh set
    foot back home. Map? 'Tis your mother waitin' at the ferry
    terminal you'll need. Mammy to take yeh by the hand an'
    show yeh the way back home.

MAURTEEN: Not been that long.

JAP: Longer even.

MAURTEEN: Said not been that long!

JAP: Fuckin' Pope's been to Ireland more times than you!

MAURTEEN: Ask me arse.

JAP: Pope an' Bill Clinton.

MAURTEEN: Oulfella's funeral, 'member?

SHAY: S'right there Jap, seven year ago, that right Maurteen?
    Went with yeh.

MAURTEEN: See?

JAP: Yeah, Frank fuckin' Sinatra, for one night only. Hello Ma,
    sorry about Da, there's a few bob, so long. Once, once in
    twelve years!

MAURTEEN: Still went back.

JAP: Anyway, funerals don't count.

MAURTEEN: Yes they do, funerals an' weddin's, that right
    Shay?

SHAY: S'right Jap. Funeral's, weddin's an' christenin's.

MAURTEEN: Births, deaths an' marriages!

JAP: No, no, no. They're not visits. They're what yeh call
    obligations.

GIT: He's right there lads.

JAP: That's duty, fella don't have no choice in them.

GIT: No choice at all.

    (*GIT looks out the window once more.*)

JAP: See.

MAURTEEN: Well I say they count.

SHAY: Me too.

JAP: Nah. Not in my book.

SHAY: Well we all don't go by your book, Jap.

JAP: More's the pity...for yous wouldn't be in the mess that yous are if you did.

MAURTEEN: How many times, then, how many times yeh set foot back, hah?

JAP: More than you. More than the lot a' yis.

MAURTEEN: 'Bout ten. Ten times since yeh cem over.

JAP: And don't I ring regular?

MAURTEEN: 'Don't I ring regular?' Hah, listen to him boys. Listen to Telegram Sam.

JAP: Every two month, rain or shine, I ring home to see how everyone is. That right Git?

GIT: S'right. I do ring with him, like. Jays cost me a bloody fortune.

MAURTEEN: Still not as good as a visit.

JAP: See me? My visits, my visits are the stuff of legend over there fella.

MAURTEEN: Yeah, the legend of the man who never cem back.

SHAY: The legend of us all.

JAP: There's folk wait for my visits they're that famous, that right Git?

MAURTEEN: The only wonder in your visitin' home Jap is that yeh ever manage to do it at all.

JAP: What would you know?

MAURTEEN: Plenty.

JAP: Yeah?

MAURTEEN: Yeah.

(*JAP takes out a packet of fags and during his following speeches uses it as a prop, a baton, as he speaks and gestures flamboyantly as he walks around the room.*)

JAP: See a real visit, a real visit Maurteen is somethin' yeh plan, work towards.

MAURTEEN: Plan! Couldn't plan a shite in a forest!
(*SHAY and GIT laugh.*)

JAP: I'm not like you mucksavages, fuckin' peasants. I don't just hop on a boat an' arrive back like that, oh no sir. See me, boy, when I visit I does it in style.

MAURTEEN: Style me arse!

JAP: Big style. Big operation.

MAURTEEN: Doesn't matter how yeh dress it up. I still been back home more than you.

JAP: A visit from Jap Kavanagh would make five a' yours.

MAURTEEN: You've a long way to go before yeh catch up on me so.

JAP: Everyone knows it's not the amount of times yeh go back but the way yeh go back, that right boys?

GIT: S'right there Maurteen, have to put on a good show.

JAP: Now yeh have it Git, now yeh have it.

GIT: Bit of a performance.

JAP: Per-fuckin'-formance! That's the word Git, performance.

MAURTEEN: Who are yeh coddin' Jap, hah, who do yeh think you're coddin' at all?

JAP: I plan it out, like I was goin' into battle.

MAURTEEN: Battle! Listen to Dan Breen lads. Battle!

(*JAP lights up his cigarette. Throughout the following the others laugh, enjoying his story telling.*)

JAP: Once I get the idea into me head I put the plan into action. Save for about three months, plenty of overtime, cut down a bit on the drink. Scrimp an' save till I've about a grand in the bank. I puts me good suit on, draws the grand out an' next thing yeh know I'm Lord Muck, King of the Irish sea.

(*Beat.*)

It brings tears to me eyes fellas. I stand at the head of the ship as it slices trough the water to take me home, large bottle in me hand an' I glarin' out ahead of me. I... I feel like a...a...a fuckin' Viking, yeh know lads, a fuckin' warrior returnin' home after long journey. Boat docks, throw me bag over the shoulder an' hop into a taxi for Hueston station. Train straight to Westport, quick drink in the town so as the word goes out; 'Jap Kavanagh's back an' his pocket's full!' Then another taxi to the Ma's an' set up camp for the next fortnight. An' for them two weeks, for them two fuckin' weeks fellas, the only time a sinner has to put a hand in his pockets is to scratch his balls. I see all the old mates, back the odd winner, ride the odd woman an' drink the townland dry.

(*A beat.*)

(*With pride.*) That Maurteen, that there's what yeh call a visit, that's how yeh show your face back home, boy.

MAURTEEN: By pretendin'? Pretendin' you're loaded, that you've made your mark? Think folk don't see through that, think they don't know the craic?

JAP: Ain't no craic about it boy, ain't no craic at all. I swear, I swear to God there do be people quein' up an' askin' for me autograph an' I boardin' the train back, me fuckin' autograph.

MAURTEEN: People aren't fools Jap, people know when you're chancin' your arm.

JAP: Hey, hey fuckin' hey now!

MAURTEEN: Playin' the big shot!

JAP: Ain't no playin'…that's me, that's me nature.

MAURTEEN: What? Coddin' you're a big success?

JAP: Ain't no failure, me.

MAURTEEN: Course yeh are, we all are. Look around yeh.

JAP: Said I ain't no failure Maurteen!

(*GIT goes over to the window and looks out again.*)

SHAY: Will you keep away from that fuckin' window you!

GIT: Thought I heard a car, okay?

SHAY: Hoppin' around like you've a ferret stuck up your arse!

(*MAURTEEN looks around at them, he gets up.*)

MAURTEEN: How long, hah, how long is it now?

JAP: What? The length of me flute?

MAURTEEN: Near thirty years since we all cem over to make our fortune. Said we'd return with it in sackfulls. The only thing now we could fill a sack with is lost chances.

JAP: That right now Mr Know-all?

MAURTEEN: Was last time I looked.

JAP: Yeah? Well yeh mustn't have looked in my sack then.

(*A beat. The others look at JAP.*)

For it's full to the brim burstin' out with jewels an' riches.

MAURTEEN: Must be robbed ones so.

JAP: Oh-ho, I've made me mark, me, don't you worry.

MAURTEEN: So?

JAP: So?

MAURTEEN: If your sack's so full what's stoppin' yeh here then?

JAP: Well yeh see, yeh see that's just it. Ain't nottin' stoppin' me here no more, ain't nottin' at all.

SHAY: Yeah?

(*JAP takes a swallow from his bottle. He has everyone's attention.*)

JAP: Sorry to break it to yis like this lads but this is me last year here. Headin' back across the Irish sea for good after Cheltenham.

GIT: Go on outta that will yeh.

MAURTEEN: Sure how many times we heard that Git? Don't be mindin' him at all.

JAP: S'true this time.

SHAY: Arra go on Jap, you're kiddin'.

JAP: Am not.

MAURTEEN: He'll never lave this place, don't mind him lads, none of us will.

JAP: Yous can stay here all your life if yis want, but not me. Told yeh when I came over it was to get enough money.

SHAY: Yeah Jap, but –

JAP: But what?

SHAY: That were nineteen seventy five, man.

JAP: Don't remember settin' a clock, do you?

SHAY: No.

JAP: Git...?

GIT: Well...no.

JAP: There yeh go then.

SHAY: An' what yeh gonna do when yeh get there?

JAP: When I get there?

SHAY: Well, yeh know...things have changed. What'll yeh do when yeh arrive?

JAP: Jaysus Shay, it's not the fuckin' moon I'm goin' to.

SHAY: Yeh know what I mean Jap. Yeh gonna head back to Drumsha?

JAP: Drumsha is it? What would I want to go back there for when there's nottin' there now bar the shell of the old house.

SHAY: And can't yeh do it up?

JAP: Sure what would I do with land at my age?

MAURTEEN: Land. Fifteen acres of prime bog.

JAP: More than your oulfella left you.

(*A pause. JAP moves away, holds the silence then:*)

Nah, boys, I'll be off to set meself up an' start me own little operation.

MAURTEEN: That right now?

JAP: S'right?

MAURTEEN: And where's the money for that comin' from?

JAP: What d'yeh mean?

MAURTEEN: Did yeh ever hear the sayin' Jap, 'When you're in a hole stopa diggin'?'

JAP: Hey! Hey fuckin' hey.

MAURTEEN: Stopa diggin', as the fella ses, an' drink your pint.

JAP: Yeh think oul Jap's a fool, don't yeh?

MAURTEEN: Didn't say that.

JAP: Think Jap's lost his way, lost the battle?

SHAY: Hey, hey. Don't be puttin' words in a fellas mouth. Maurteen said nottin' like that at all.

JAP: Well let me tell you me oul flower, Jap Kavanagh looked after his pounds, shillin's an' pence an' he over here, got that?

GIT: Well dig out some of them pounds, shillin's an' pence an' buy a round will yeh?

JAP: Hey now, hey now Git! Fuckin' serious boy.

GIT: Only jokin' Jap, jaysus, only jokin'.

MAURTEEN: Jaysus, relax will yeh?

SHAY: Serious Jap?

JAP: Hah?

SHAY: Yeh really doin' it, goin' back?

JAP: Have to go home sometime Shay, what? I mean, none of us came over for good.

(*A pause as JAP scans the faces.*)

Hah? hah? Mean, we was boys an' we cem here first, boys. Now look at us, old fuckin' men nearly.

GIT: Hey. Hey fuckin' hey Jap. No oul lad me, speak for yourself. Still got me looks, still pull the women. Old fuckin' men!

JAP: I'm serious Git…we're gettin' on, all of us. S'alright for Maurteen an' Shay, they've settled down, have a family. Us bucks, what are we to do?

SHAY: You've a woman too.

JAP: Agh…!

SHAY: And a daycent one at that.

JAP: Want kids, gang 'a kids.

SHAY: And what's wrong with Shirley…she'd give yeh a hurlin' team that one if yeh got her to move in with yeh.

GIT: An' where would I go if she did?

(*JAP looks at SHAY, not so much a glare but sufficient for GIT to look away. MAURTEEN sniggers.*)

JAP: You tryin' to be funny?

SHAY: Huh?

JAP: Said are you tryin' to be funny?

SHAY: Hey. Alright? Didn't mean nottin', okay?

JAP: Ain't no racist me but…yeh know…yeh know, want me kids to look like me.

(*GIT raises his glass.*)

GIT: Well Jap, here's to yeh, never thought I'd see the day.

JAP: So how about it Git, me an' you?

GIT: Me an' you?

JAP: You don't wanna stay over here for ever do yeh?

GIT: Over here, in this cold kip? Are yeh mad?

JAP: Well then?

(*A beat.*)

GIT: Bit sudden, isn't it?

JAP: Don't go now Git an' we'll never. Look at poor Jackie, shipped across in a wooden box, not enough at the mass to fill a funeral car… I don't want that. None of us want that.

GIT: An' what'd I do when I got there? Ain't got no sack a' riches, me.

JAP: Would yeh listen to him lads, best chippy in London this fella an' he wonderin' what he'll do back home, would yeh stop.

GIT: S'no joke Jap. Can't just arrive back in Ireland with a bag a' tools.

JAP: Why not?

GIT: Just can't, that's why.

JAP: Look, when yeh cem over here did yeh know what yeh were goin' to do?

GIT: Well, not really I suppose.

JAP: Well...it's just the same an' yeh goin' home. Like startin' all over again.

GIT: (*Trying to make light of it, jokingly.*) Well I'm definitely not goin' back so! Fuck that, the shit, the abuse we went through.

JAP: That's only 'cause we were Paddies.

GIT: An' what'll we be back over there?

JAP: Hah?

GIT: We'll be as much strange fish over there as we were an' we settin' foot off'a the boat here for the first time.

JAP: Hang on Git, maybe I've confused yeh. It's Ireland I'm talkin' about, not Timbuck-fuckin'-too!

GIT: It's another country Jap...different one entirely than the one we left behind yeh know.

JAP: 'Tis not.

SHAY: He's right. You'll be like headless chickens over there now.

GIT: Fellas like me an' you...it'd be like goin' to...to Brussels or somethin'.

JAP: Brussels?

GIT: Sure the money an' all's different over there. S'all Euros, Ecus, bollox to all that I'm still tryin' to get over the shock of the ten bob note goin'

JAP: Jaysus Christ, would yeh listen to this whinger.

GIT: S'not the same place we left, s'all I'm sayin'.

JAP: Then won't it be another adventure, 'nother journey into the unknown?

GIT: Too old for journeys, too old for the unknown.

JAP: Come on Git...me an' you, hah? Me an' you. They say there's a lotta gold over in that island now, lotta gold needs a diggin'. I've still two strong hands, you too.

GIT: I'll eh, I'll think about it, hah?

JAP: Think all yeh want. But one thing's for sure Jap Kavanagh's takin' the B&I boat back after he clears up at Cheltenham, another country or not.

(A silence. SHAY gets up and goes to the jukebox.)

SHAY: Jaysus, where would yeh get it, not a rebel song on it anywhere. What, did we have to decommission them too? I remember the day there'd be nothin' but rebel songs on that yoke.

GIT: A few more of these boys into me an' you'll have all the rebel songs yeh want Shay-boy.

(JAP lets out a roar, it spurs the others on, makes them excited for a moment.)

JAP: Yup!

SHAY: Hey!

GIT: Any rebel song yeh want boy!

JAP: Up the IRA!

SHAY: Hey fuckin' hey, I said!

(GIT looks at him.)

GIT: What?

SHAY: No fuckin' Shay-boy, alright Git?

JAP: Hey.

SHAY: No fuckin' Shay-boy, alright? The name's Shay.

GIT: Fuck sake man...okay? Jaysus...

MAURTEEN: That a car now?

(The noise of a car sends GIT Running to a door.)

GIT: Hey, hey. Here we go boys, here we go!

(GIT exits.)

JAP: Look at him, like a little lap dog.

SHAY: He's just excited, that's all. Aren't yeh lookin' forward to seein' the big man?

JAP: I'm easy.

MAURTEEN: 'Course he's lookin' forward to seein' him.

JAP: If...if he shows up.

SHAY: The big man'll show up, don't you worry.

MAURTEEN: Yeah well he better do it soon, for I'm not waitin' all day.

JAP: Under orders, are yeh?

MAURTEEN: Five more minutes an' I'm off.

JAP: Jaysus, some friend you are. Only got here.

MAURTEEN: Yeah, well at least I showed up at the mass, didn't I?

(JAP takes out some fags, he puts one in his mouth the

holds the pack out to MAURTEEN, MAURTEEN looks
at them for a moment then takes one.)

JAP: Jesus, it was a bad turn out wasn't it?

SHAY: There'll be a better one back home.

JAP: Wait'll I see some of the others.

SHAY: Lave it.

JAP: Too mean, that's what, too mean to take the day off work
to pay a bit of respect.

SHAY: It's time's like these when you find out who your true
friends are.

JAP: Now you have it, now you have it Shay.

*(GIT returns, the others look to him trying not to show
their hope. He shakes his head.)*

GIT: Maybe...maybe he's taken a wrong turn.

MAURTEEN: Wrong turn, jaysus, that's a good one, wrong
turn. That man could find his way here an' he blindfolded.

GIT: You sure yeh left word where we were meetin'?

MAURTEEN: Want me to tattoo it onto me forehead? How
many more times more are yeh gonna ask me that Git?

GIT: Just that-well, yeh know...s'not like the big man, s'not
like him at all lads.

JAP: Maybe, maybe he never got the message, himself and his
poxy answerin' machine.

MAURTEEN: Arra jaysus sake!

JAP: Will you stop bein' so snippy!

MAURTEEN: Call a spade a spade will yous? The man's not
comin', alright?

(A silence falls.)

Big fat bastard! Didn't even come to the church for jaysus
sake, yeh hardly expect him to come here now do yeh?

GIT: Jaysus, it'll be terrible if he didn't get the message.

MAURTEEN: Look, he knows. Alright? Jaysus, wasn't the
poor whore's death all over the papers?

(Beat.)

Not even a wreath from him, a mass card even!

JAP: Bastard.

(A silence falls.)

SHAY: Still can't believe he's gone lads.

GIT: Jaysus, this day last week we were all havin' a great time, what?

SHAY: Little did we know.

GIT: Little did we know.

JAP: Never know what's around the corner.

SHAY: All his...you know, all his stuff gone back?

GIT: Wasn't that much of it. Few photos, letters, the good suit he had went on him in the coffin.

JAP: For all anyone saw of him. Jaysus, but you'd think they'd let us have one last look at him, hah, one last goodbye.

GIT: Wasn't a sight for no man to set eyes on Jap, sight for no man.

(*MAURTEEN finishes off his drink. He slams his glass down on the table.*)

MAURTEEN: Well boys... I'll lave yis to it.

JAP: Hey!

MAURTEEN: See yeh in a few weeks maybe.

JAP: Hey, hey hold on now.

MAURTEEN: Said five minutes Jap.

JAP: Yeah, two poxy minutes ago!

SHAY: Arra come on, yeh can't go Maurteen, we just got here.

MAURTEEN: Sorry fellas...

GIT: Arra jaysus man...for Jackie.

SHAY: Come on Maurteen.

MAURTEEN: Look I'm not much company today lads.

JAP: Well that's great, so it is.

MAURTEEN: He'll get a good send off with yourselves.

JAP: I say that's fuckin' great altogether!

MAURTEEN: Look I told yis I wouldn't be sayin' long an' we lavin' the church, didn't I?

(*A silence as MAURTEEN puts on his coat.*)

SHAY: Maybe see yeh in The Lion later? S'where we'll probably end up tonight.

MAURTEEN: I'm gonna knock The Lion on the head for a while I think Shay.

JAP: An' what about our Saturday's?

MAURTEEN: What about them?

JAP: You'll still come won't yeh?

MAURTEEN: Sure what'll be the point?

JAP: Well you're hardly goin' off the drink for the rest of your life, are yeh?

MAURTEEN: Dunno.

JAP: Jaysus sake man. What are yeh savin' up for a kitchen for whole street?

MAURTEEN: Look, maybe the odd Saturday, I dunno, see how it goes.

JAP: Gonna break up the gang Maurteen, break up the gang if you start this carry on.

SHAY: Don't be talkin' stupid you.

MAURTEEN: Yous'll manage alright without me.

SHAY: A game of pool or somethin'? Doesn't have to be a drink.

MAURTEEN: Yeah pool, a game a pool'd go down well.

SHAY: There yeh go then.

GIT: Later in The Lion, Maurteen? Just for an hour even?

MAURTEEN: Maybe, I'll see, Git.

(*MAURTEEN makes his way to the door.*)

JAP: Jaysus, it's bad enough you're off the drink but does that mean yeh have to stop buyin' it too?

(*MAURTEEN stops, he scans the faces.*)

GIT: Look the man wants to go Jap.

JAP: He can still find time to buy his mates a drink can't he? Specially if it's gonna be the last.

GIT: Don't be mindin' him Maurteen, off yeh go.

MAURTEEN: D'yis want a drink off'a me?

SHAY: Go on will yeh, he's only jossin' with yeh. Aren't yeh Jap?

(*A stand off, they look at each other.*)

JAP: Go on if you're goin' so.

MAURTEEN: I'll get the round in, alright?

(*The others mumble and nod their heads.*)

SHAY: Good man Maurteen, another five minutes won't kill yeh.

JAP: No, but another lemonade will.

(*JAP laughs, MAURTEEN joins in with him. A little ice has broken.*)

MAURTEEN: Go on, another five minutes so. An' I swear, if he's not here by then...

(MAURTEEN exits to get the drinks.)

SHAY: Must be hard.

JAP: What?

SHAY: No easy thing stayin' off the drink an' everyone 'round
yeh throwin' them back.

JAP: Savin' up for a kitchen me hole.

SHAY: Lotta money for a kitchen nowadays Jap, lotta money.

JAP: He wasn't savin' up for a kitchen an' he out with us the
other night, was he?

SHAY: Hey.

JAP: Yeh know what I'm sayin' Shay? Bit sudden.

SHAY: Look Jap, yeh don't know what the story is, okay?
Let's leave it at that?

(A beat. SHAY walks away, JAP watches him.)

JAP: Hey…

GIT: Don't be pushin' the man for a reason, will yeh not?

JAP: Here, Shay… You know somethin'.

SHAY: Jap, fuck off.

JAP: Gitna…?

(GIT puts his hands up in the air.)

GIT: Hey now.

*(JAP looks at them for a moment, convinced they know
something.)*

JAP: Hey-fuckin'-hey boys!

GIT: Will yeh lave things be man, hah?

JAP: Yous keepin' somethin' from me, hah?

SHAY: Someone stick on another tune, will they?

JAP: Fuck another tune! Yous know somethin'.

GIT: Jap, fuck's sake man, keep it down, will yeh? You'll only
upset him.

JAP: What did he do? Hah…what did he do Git?

(SHAY goes to the jukebox and looks at it.)

I don't fuckin' believe it!

SHAY: Didn't open me mouth.

JAP: Jaysus Christ, jaysus Christ almighty!

GIT: Come on, leave it out Jap.

JAP: When?

SHAY: When what?

GIT: Look, s'not fair what you're askin' Jap.

JAP: Yous know boys, yous fuckin' know!

SHAY: It's nothin' to do with us, right?

JAP: How bad this time, hah?

SHAY: Jaysus man will yeh give it a rest?

JAP: S'not on boys, s'not on at all that crack.

SHAY: I'm sorry I opened me mouth, sorry I opened me fuckin' mouth!

(A pause. GIT crosses and looks out a window. JAP shakes his head and lights another smoke. He exhales a large cloud of smoke out long and hard.)

GIT: Plane should have landed by now, what?

JAP: Huh?

GIT: Jackie's plane, should've landed in Ireland by now.

JAP: Near enough.

(SHAY joins GIT at the window.)

SHAY: We should've gone over with it boys.

GIT: I know.

JAP: What?

SHAY: S'not right Jap. Should've gone over with him. His last journey.

JAP: Flap our arms an' fly over yeh mean?

SHAY: What we'll drink here today would've paid for a seat on the plane.

JAP: An' what would we drink over there, tap water? Wouldn't we look lovely in front of everyone sittin' like four statues hopin' someone'd fire a few pints into us.

SHAY: Everything's not a public appearance Jap, we're not fuckin' celebrities yeh know!

JAP: No use goin' over without a tosser in your pocket. Yeh have to look the part.

(This comment causes GIT to stare at JAP. But his reply is cut short by SHAY.)

GIT: I thought yeh said you'd rakes of money?

SHAY: Bollix the part! We should be at his burial, s'only right, so it is. Should be there throwin' a handful of earth in on him an' sayin' goodbye proper.

GIT: Hey…hey that's it boys!

SHAY: What he would've wanted.

GIT: Big Joe! Maybe the big man went back home for the burial? I mean, he has the shekels for it.

JAP: Has the shekels to bring us all over.

SHAY: Jays, never thought of that one. Never thought of that one at all Git.

GIT: Bet yeh, bet yeh that's what the bastard did. Got the plane to Knock, hired a car an' went to the burial. Jaysus, he's a dark horse that fella, that's all I can say, a dark horse.

JAP: Well if he did I'm finished with him.

GIT: Hah?

JAP: Doin' that an' not tellin' us about it. Not on. Mean if he went over he should've brought us with him. I mean four plane tickets wouldn't have killed, hah…hah?

SHAY: I won't argue with that.

(MAURTEEN returns with the drinks. He sets them out.)

MAURTEEN: Happy now?

(JAP looks at him accusingly.)

What's up with yeh now?

JAP: Not a bother on me.

MAURTEEN: Then what's the long face for?

(A pause as MAURTEEN puts the drinks out.)

JAP: How's the misses?

MAURTEEN: Hah?

JAP: Maggie. How's she keepin'?

MAURTEEN: She's sound, sound.

JAP: Good, I'm glad to hear it, glad to hear she's okay. Not a bother on her. Very fond of Maggie, know? Don't like hearin' that she's not well.

(MAURTEEN doesn't like JAP's tone.)

MAURTEEN: That right now?

JAP: Tell her I was askin' for her.

MAURTEEN: Yeah, will.

JAP: Good.

(MAURTEEN stares at him.)

GIT: Come on lads…

MAURTEEN: Spit it out cunty-fuck.

JAP: Hey… Just askin' how the hen is, not a problem is it? Not against the law?

(A silence. JAP sips his drink. MAURTEEN watches him.)

MAURTEEN: How's the coon?

GIT: Jaysus man!

(JAP jumps up. SHAY comes between them.)

SHAY: Hey, fuck Maurteen, steady there Jap-jays Maurteen, what the fuck boy, I mean what the fuck way is that to talk about a man's woman, hah?

JAP: At least the black eyes she has are the ones she was born with.

GIT: Will you lave it out Jap!

(MAURTEEN looks at SHAY.)

SHAY: Don't be lookin' at me, didn't open me mouth, okay?

GIT: Jaysus sake boys…we're here to remember Jackie remember, not start this shite.

SHAY: Come on boys, shake hands, hah?

(MAURTEEN holds his hand out.)

MAURTEEN: Sorry Jap…didn't mean to call her a coon.

(Beat.)

Meant the big black nigger bitch you're ridin'.

JAP: That's fuckin' it!

(JAP dives on MAURTEEN. They roll along the floor, grunting and punching. GIT and SHAY try to pull them apart. Ad-libbing 'Break it up's and 'fuck sake's. Eventually SHAY pulls JAP away, GIT holds MAURTEEN.)

Should be ashamed of yourself, baitin' a woman like that.

MAURTEEN: An' you've never raised your hand to a woman before?

GIT: Come on now lads.

JAP: Not at the rate you do. It's like a fuckin' sport to you, a fuckin' past time!

MAURTEEN: Look, it wasn't my fault, okay?

JAP: An' who's fault was it, mine, Git's, Shay's?

MAURTEEN: I was drunk, alright. Was an accident.

JAP: Drunk? Drunk! What sort of an excuse is that, sure we all get drunk.

MAURTEEN: I wasn't meself after hearin' 'bout Jackie.

JAP: None of us were.

SHAY: Jaysus sake Jap, lave the man be, will yeh?

JAP: Don't mean we go home an' knock seven shades of shite

out of our hens.

MAURTEEN: It was a mistake, alright? Won't happen again, okay?

JAP: Yeah, an' how many times have we heard that song, hah, how many times?

GIT: Come on Jap, remember the day that's in it.

JAP: That's a fuckin' lady you're married to fella.

(*MAURTEEN starts to feel the strain.*)

MAURTEEN: I… I know.

JAP: Fuckin' lady not a fuckin' punchbag!

MAURTEEN: Hey, alright Jap, okay?

GIT: Take it easy Jap, will yeh?

JAP: Not on Maurteen.

SHAY: Come on Jap, sit down and let it go.

(*SHAY leads JAP to a seat.*)

JAP: Not on at all, s'all I'm sayin'.

MAURTEEN: Think I don't know that? Think I don't care? Why the fuck d'yeh think I'm sittin' here drinkin' this? Think I enjoy it, like the taste?

GIT: You're doin' the right thing Maurteen.

SHAY: The man's makin' an effort Jap, what more d'yeh want?

MAURTEEN: AA. A fuckin' A boys, that's how serious I am, alright?

SHAY: AA. Jap, what more proof do yeh want, hah?

MAURTEEN: An' it's not easy, yeh hear?

GIT: One step at a time, that right Maurteen?

SHAY: One step at a time Jap.

JAP: You mean…you've, you've joined?

MAURTEEN: Well, not yet, but I am, gonna ring them to-morrow, sort it all out.

JAP: Arra fuck!

MAURTEEN: Honest, I swear! I'm gonna sort me drinkin' out once and for all.

GIT: Fair play to you.

MAURTEEN: It's…it's just hard, know what I mean, take time.

SHAY: Least you're makin' an effort. There's fellas wouldn't give a shite what they did an' they drunk, wouldn't bat an eyelid.

(*A silence, MAURTEEN crosses across and sits on his own.
He lights a smoke.*)

MAURTEEN: That fuckin' rum! Jaysus, when I drinks fuckin' rum!

JAP: Well don't drink the fuckin' piss then!

MAURTEEN: Never, s'long as I live there won't be another drop a' rum passin' my lips. Any a' you fellas ever see me drinkin' so much as a drop a' rum pick up a stool an' crash it down over me head, yeh hear? Smash it over me skull like you were puttin' a sledge to a wall.

(*A beat. JAP has calmed down, his tone changes.*)

JAP: She...she alright?

MAURTEEN: Grand.

JAP: Sure?

MAURTEEN: Just a little cut over her eyes.

JAP: Jaysus!

SHAY: Hey.

MAURTEEN: A small one, nothin' big like, just a...a graze like.

JAP: You're gonna loose that woman Maurteen, know that?
(*MAURTEEN nods his head.*)
Gonna loose her an' the kids once and for all.

MAURTEEN: Look, it won't happen again, okay?
(*A silence falls for a moment.*)
Look, eh, I'm... I'm sorry for sayin' that Jap, 'bout Shirley.

JAP: Forget about it.

MAURTEEN: No, wasn't right, not on at all that talk. I'm sorry. She's a grand girl...one of the best.
(*JAP raises his hand, apology accepted. A longer silence.
SHAY tries to get a bit of energy into the sagging atmosphere.*)

GIT: Here come on lads, what sort of a fuckin' wake is this, hah? This is Jackie Flavin's day, now who's gonna start off with the sing song, what? Come on Jap, The Bold fenian men.

JAP: Nah, fuck it. Think I'll eh, think I'll head off meself boys.

GIT: Agh for the love of jaysus!

JAP: Arra, what's the point, stuck out here in the side room of the club? It's in at the bar we should be, in at the bar.

GIT: Jackie... Jackie Flavin's the point. Now come on lads, Shay, Shay, give us Kevin Barry.

SHAY: Agh...

GIT: Maurteen... Maurteen you start if off.

MAURTEEN: I'm not in the mood for singing, Git.

GIT: Well I'll sing. I'll sing for Jackie. 'Far away from the land of the shamrock and heather. In search of a living in Exile we roam. But when ever we chance to assemble together we sing of country we once called our home.'

(Suddenly a voice from off.)

JOE: Sure there was only one of us that could do justice to that song...

(A man appears at the door, JOE MULLEN.)

...an' he's dead God love him.

(All are surprised and even delighted to see him even if they don't entirely show it.)

SHAY: Well jaysus Christ!

JAP: Joe Mullen! How's she cuttin'?

JOE: Could be worse.

GIT: About shaggin' time, Joe, about shaggin' time!

(JOE raises his two arms up in the air in apology.)

JOE: I know, I know, I know.

(An awkward silence. JOE senses it.)

Everythin' alright lads?

GIT: Course, we were just about to start the sing song, that right lads?

JAP: We were givin' up on you.

JOE: Well I'm here now, huh?

(Beat.)

So how are yeh boys?

GIT: Sure we're grand, all grand, aren't we lads?

JOE: Good, good. An' how are the women...hah, how are the girls?

SHAY: Still there, still keepin' us on our toes.

JOE: Sorry I couldn't get to the service, a little bit of bother on one of the sites.

GIT: Sure you're here now Joe, that's all that matters, what lads?

JOE: God but it's been a bit of a while, what? Sometime since we were all together like this.

JAP: Thought you'd forgotten about us.

JOE: Sure how could I do that? I say, how could I do that, what?

MAURTEEN: You're lookin' well Joseph.

JOE: Arra, I'm not here for compliments Maurteen. It's poor Jackie our praises should be on now, God rest his soul.
(*JOE blesses himself the others follow and mumble a 'God rest him'.*)
A sad day an' us all meetin' up like this, what?

JAP: A black day.

GIT: Tragedy.

JOE: Of the highest order.
(*An awkward silence.*)
Was there a good turn out at the service boys?

JAP: Mass, Joe, mass…

SHAY: Jackie, kept himself to himself Joe, yeh know the way it was.

JOE: I do, I do. And everythin' was looked after?

SHAY: His father flew over an' took care of all the arrangements.

JOE: Oul Mickser, God love him. Must be what, seventy odd by now.

GIT: Near enough.

JOE: They say it's an awful thing for a parent to bury a child.
(*The following three responses are said together.*)

SHAY: Tis, tis.

MAURTEEN: Desperate.

GIT: Shocking altogether.

JAP: He was eh, he was askin' for yeh.

JOE: He was?

JAP: Says he, 'Tell, Joe Mullen I said hello.'

JOE: Did he now? I must, I say, I must send him a card, send him my condolences.

JAP: Make sure yeh do.

(*There is a silence for a moment.*)

GIT: God, that poor man's heart.

SHAY: T'was well yeh weren't there Joe.

JOE: Sad, was it?

SHAY: Sad isn't the word.

GIT: Wouldn't let go the coffin, poor Mickser. He'd his arms
    wrapped round it an' the tears, jaysus the tears spillin'
    down off'a his cheeks an' onto the wood. 'Why?' he ses,
    'Why did he not come home? Was he afraid we'd think less
    of him 'cause he never made anythin' of himself?'

JOE: God love him.

GIT: He looked at us all an' said we should all go back home
    before the same thing happens to us.

JOE: Huh?

JAP: (*Snaps at GIT.*) Hey.

JOE: What thing?

JAP: Don't mind him Joe.

JOE: What thing Git?

JAP: Nottin'!

GIT: I was there, Jap, I was fuckin' there!

JOE: Where? What?

JAP: An' yeh were drunk too.

GIT: Look –

JAP: (*Changing the subject.*) So, how's business Joe?

JOE: Well now, to tell yeh the truth Jap, 'tis not too bad,
    I say, not too bad at all.

JAP: How many is it now you've got workin' for yeh?

JOE: Twelve men.

JAP: Twelve men.

SHAY: Jays, you're doing well.

JAP: Would we know any of them?

JOE: Eh, I wouldn't say so… Jocks most of them.

JAP: Jocks?

JOE: Yeah, yeh know, Scotsmen?

JAP: (*A little menacing in his response.*) I know what a fuckin'
    Jock is, you mean you've no Paddies workin' for yeh?

JOE: D'yeh know they way it is Jap? But yeh can't get them!

Can't get a good Paddy in this town for love or money.

(*JAP doesn't buy JOE's answer but lets it go.*)

SHAY: Leave it to us, what?

JOE: You'd sooner find gold up the high hole of your arse than get a good Paddy.

SHAY: (*Raising his glass.*) The fuckin' Paddies!

(*The others share in the toast.*)

ALL: The Paddies.

MAURTEEN: Fuck the Paddies.

(*A silence. MAURTEEN raises his glass.*)

MAURTEEN: To Jackie Flavin.

ALL: Jackie Flavin.

(*They all raise their glasses and drink back. A pause.*)

JOE: Still can't believe it lads, still can't believe it.

SHAY: We was all out drinkin' with him that evenin'. That right lads?

JOE: And how was he?

GIT: Not a bother. He was after sendin' the few bob across to the mother when I met him.

JOE: Jaysus, he never let that woman down, what boys, never.

SHAY: Hail, rain or shine there was a postal order sent home every fortnight.

JOE: Well we'll give him a good wake, what fellas?

SHAY: That we will.

(*JOE deepens his voice, clenches his fist and speaks slowly.*)

JOE: A good fuckin' wake!

GIT: You fuckin' said it Joe, you fuckin' said it boy!

(*JOE takes off his coat and flings across a chair, he claps his hands and speaks in an excited tone.*)

JOE: Now I hope yous all cancelled your plans. For today is a day for drinkin'! We'll have a good sup here first then off to The Lion what?

JAP: Now you're talkin'!

GIT: Come on the drink!

JOE: And today is on me fellas, hear that…on fuckin' me!

(*JAP roars out in excitement as if commencing battle. He rubs his hands.*)

JAP: Come on yeh boy yeh!

JOE: Now come on lads…what are yis havin'? Jap?

JAP: Whiskey!

JOE: Whiskey it is! Shay?

SHAY: Fuck it me too Joe!

JOE: Yes sir! Gitna?

GIT: Dammit I'll have a whiskey too!

JOE: Whiskey all round so boys.

MAURTEEN: Joe.

(As JOE goes off to get them MAURTEEN calls him. JOE stops.)

JOE: I haven't forgotten Maurteen, Jamaican rum.

MAURTEEN: No, no…a lemonade'll do me.

JOE: Hah! D'you hear this fella, lemonade! Hah!

MAURTEEN: Serious Joe, a lemonade'll do.

JOE: What?

JAP: He's…he's on tablets, that right Maurteen. Doctors orders, no drink.

MAURTEEN: That's the way.

JOE: Oh, I see. Fair enough so, lemonade it is Maurteen.

GIT: Here Joe, make mine a large one, will yeh?

(As JOE goes out to order.)

JOE: Large one, fuck a large one we'll have a bottle and when that's gone another to wash it down!

JAP: Come on yeh boy-yeh Joe, come on yeh boy-yeh!

SHAY: Fair play to the big man!

JAP: Jaysus, but I'm in form for a session today boys!

GIT: Here's your brother.

JAP: I'm gonna drink for Ireland today!

SHAY: North an' South!

JAP: North an' fuckin' South, you said it Shay!

(MAURTEEN is sitting alone biting his nails, he is in some distress, although quietly.)

SHAY: There'll be no work in the mornin'.

JAP: Are yeh mad? Not a fuckin' tap'll be done!

SHAY: Sure we'll take the week off, what lads?

JAP: Jaysus, but yeh know I might just do that. What do you think, Git?

(GIT looks a little uncomfortably at JAP.)

SHAY: What ails yeh Git? Afraid you'll get sacked?

GIT: Yeh know how it is boys.

JAP: Of course we'll take the day off, the whole fuckin' week if we like, amn't I the foreman?

GIT: We'll see boys, we'll see.

SHAY: Go on yeh oul sissy yeh!

JAP: He's sayin' that now Shay, you wait till he's hung over in the mornin'. It'll be another story then, what?

SHAY: What about yourself Maurteen…the week off work?

MAURTEEN: (*With a smile on his face.*) An' die of lemonade poisonin' into the bargain?

(*They all burst out laughing and drink back their pints. MAURTEEN takes out a cigarette from a pack, his hands are shaking, he lets the fags fall and struggles to pick them up, everyone observes this.*)

JAP: You okay skipper?

MAURTEEN: Fuckin' hands…

(*As MAURTEEN tries to light his fag we see his hands shake. He is embarrassed but tries to make light of it.*)

Jaysus, what ails me at all?

JAP: Not healthy givin' up the drink like that. Man should do it slowly, cut down like.

MAURTEEN: I'll be alright.

JAP: Shandy even.

MAURTEEN: Shandy?

JAP: Just to take the edge off'a yeh, s'all.

MAURTEEN: I'll be grand, grand.

(*MAURTEEN gets up and walks around, he begins biting at his nails and spitting them out. We see he is finding the strain to stay off the drink more and more difficult.*)

GIT: Maybe yeh should, yeh know, go home?

MAURTEEN: And Joe just after arrivin'? I'll be grand.

JAP: I'm tellin' yeh, shandy's the man. Won't get yeh drunk an' it won't lave yeh sober, just a little soft spot in the middle.

SHAY: A pint a' shandy's the man alright. Least you'll have a pint in your hand, know? Won't seem as bad that'a way.
(*MAURTEEN pauses.*)

MAURTEEN: Fuck it lads but can't I give it up in the mornin', hah?

(*GIT gives SHAY a look, SHAY shrugs his shoulders.*)

JAP: This mornin', tomorrow mornin', what's the difference, hah?

MAURTEEN: I mean, s'not right, is it, s'not right for poor oul Jackie, is it?

JAP: You'll be grand Maurteen. We'll keep an' eye on yeh.

MAURTEEN: Now hear me, I'm only havin' the few, alright?

JAP: Hear that now boys, the man's just havin' the few.

MAURTEEN: An' I'll take me time, so don't go fillin' me glass up.

JAP: Pace yourself Maurteen, that's the secret. S'all about pace.

SHAY: Man could drink for two days if he paced himself proper, two days solid.

JAP: Haven't I done it often enough meself?

(*MAURTEEN drains his lemonade back then calls out.*)

MAURTEEN: Go on Joe, fuck that piss, I'll have a lager shandy so!

JAP: Go on yeh boy yeh!

GIT: I told yeh he'd come, hah, hah? Didn't I tell you he'd come…and he's payin' for the day too!

SHAY: Now come on Gitna…give us a song!

GIT: What'll it be?

JAP: Anythin' once there's a dead Brit in it. For we've songs enough full of our own dead.

GIT: We'll be here for a week so!

SHAY: (*Letting out a roar.*) Come on Gitna!

JAP: (*Spurred on by SHAY he roars.*) Up the 'Ra!

(*GIT bursts into song. JAP starts to stamp his feet to the beat, SHAY joins in.*)

GIT: 'Go on home English soldier, go on home. Have yeh got no fuckin' country of your own. For eight hundred years we fought yeh without fear an' we'll fight yeh for eight hundred more.'

(*JAP puts his arm around SHAY's shoulder and the two join in the singing and stomping. Throughout the following JOE returns carrying a bottle of whiskey and a tray of glasses and swaying his shoulders to the beat of the song as*

39

they all join in with GIT.)

'We got best part of you out in twenty one.'

ALL: 'Twenty one!'

GIT: 'You left faster than a bullet from a gun.'

ALL: 'From a gun!'

GIT: 'But now the time's at hand to redeem our native land and drive your filthy vermin from our shores.'

ALL: 'Go on home English soldier, go on home. Have yeh got no fuckin' country of your own. For eight hundred years we fought yeh without fear an' we'll fight yeh for eight hundred more.'

(*Sudden blackout, silence.*)

End of Act One.

ACT TWO

About an hour later. The bottle of whiskey, almost empty, stands beside a jug of water on a table. On another is a tray and the remnants of sandwiches, crusts etc.

Jackets are off, sleeves rolled up. The oiled hair of some of the men is now hanging over their foreheads and eyes. <u>None of the men are pissed drunk</u>. They are well able to hold their drink.

JAP and JOE are carrying MAURTEEN on their shoulders, MAURTEEN is full back on the drink and has a glass of whiskey in his hand. His shirt is lying on the floor and he is in his vest. He comes to the end of the song.

MAURTEEN: 'God's curse on you England, you cruel heartless monsters, your deeds they would shame all the demons in hell. There are no flowers blooming but the shamrock is growing on the grave of James Connolly, the Irish rebel.'
(*All burst into a round of applause and cheering. MAURTEEN gets down from the shoulders, sweeping his hair back over his head.*)

JOE: Yeh never lost it Maurteen, never lost it boy!

JAP: Yeh could sing for Ireland Maurteen.

GIT: Sing for Ireland!

SHAY: Jaysus boys, but he's gettin' some send off, what?

JAP: We're only gettin' started Shay, only gettin' warmed up.

SHAY: Right, who's turn is it?

JOE: I've sang.

JAP: Gitna…?

MAURTEEN: Git… Banna Strand.

SHAY: The lonely Banna Strand!
(*GIT gets up and heads out towards the toilets.*)

GIT: Have to drain the vein first lads.

JOE: (*Stuffing a sandwich in his mouth.*) Git ask her for another plate a' sandwiches an' another bottle of Jemmy on your way out will yeh?

GIT: Comin' right up.

(*GIT exits. SHAY calls after him.*)

SHAY: An' another jug a' water too.

JAP: Them sandwiches were a great idea Joe.

SHAY: Nottin' like a bit a' soakage for the drink, what?

JAP: We'll last all day doin' this.

JOE: That's the intention, boys. That's the intention.

(*MAURTEEN pours another glass of whiskey and shoves a sandwich in his mouth.*)

MAURTEEN: Fair play to yeh Joe. Put it there.

(*They shake hands.*)

I love this fella, know that? Love this fucker. I do... you're one of the best, isn't he lads, one of the best?

(*SHAY goes to him.*)

SHAY: Put it there mucker! Put. It. There.

(*They shake hands. We see JAP isn't particularly enjoying all this.*)

One of the best is right.

JOE: Now, now lads.

SHAY: No I mean it, credit where credit's due. You're doin' Jackie proud buyin' the drink an' food like that, isn't he lads?

MAURTEEN: Daycent man.

JAP: Sure isn't it the least he could do, hah?

(*JOE smiles weakly at this, not sure of JAP's intention. They hold each other's gaze.*)

Yeah...yeah.

MAURTEEN: Good to see things are on the up an' up for yeh Joe, isn't it Shay?

JOE: The only way is up, I say the only way is up, what lads?

SHAY: Fair play to yeh Joe, always knew you'd do it. Always said if there was one of us that would make our mark it would be Joe Mullen.

JAP: Don't remember yeh sayin' that.

SHAY: Them's the very words I used.

JAP: Do you remember him sayin' that Maurteen?

MAURTEEN: Hah?

JOE: (*Breaking in.*) Sure we've all done well, what? Nice home, families.

JAP: Would yeh listen to this fella tryin' to be modest? 'All done well!'

JOE: Well yis have, haven't yis, in your own way like.

JAP: Not done as well as yourself, that's for sure.

JOE: Dunno Jap, still have to get up out a' me bed in the
mornin' same as any a' yous.

JAP: Yeah but you're a boss man, gaffer! Mornin' come an'
you don't like the look-of it…well, I'd say you just grab
them covers an' curl right up like a baby an' get one a'
your Jocks to look after things.

JOE: I wish. D'yeh know the way it is Jap, but the more men
yeh have under yeh the more yeh have to keep an eye on
things.

JAP: Ever hear of a foreman?

JOE: Ten a penny…it's the ones you can trust that are hard to
find.

JAP: Maybe they're hard to find because you've never looked
in the right place?

*(Another stand off. SHAY breaks the ice, pouring a glass
of whiskey out and handing it to JOE.)*

SHAY: Yeh done us proud Joe, we're all proud of yeh, that
right Jap?

JAP: I'm bitter of no man.

JOE: Your day'll come lads, mark my words.

JAP: Amn't I sick tellin' them that?

JOE: Just a matter of grabbin' the bull by the horns and
hangin' on.

JAP: The bull by the horns…now you have it.

*(JAP takes up a sandwich and munches on it as he looks
at the records on the jukebox.)*

JOE: How's all the kids fellas?

MAURTEEN: Not a bother.

JOE: Still the four is it Shay?

SHAY: Four is enough.

JOE: What is it you have now Maurteen?

MAURTEEN: Six.

JOE: Six! Jaysus, a fuckin' stallion we have here fellas, a
fuckin' stallion.

MAURTEEN: And I'm not finished yet!

43

JOE: Jays, he's some man for one man, what lads?

JAP: Six kids is nottin'! Jays when I get a girl she'll have six in the first few years.

SHAY: Can't.

JAP: Hah?

SHAY: Can't have six in a few years, takes a least five years to have five.

JAP: Ever hear a twins?

SHAY: All I'm sayin' is –

JAP: Tis seven or eight kids I'll be lookin' from off a women.

SHAY: Well you'll want to start using the lad fairly rapid so, won't you?

JOE: So how's the work lads?

MAURTEEN: Ah, you know yourself.

JAP: Work's grand…all makin' a fortune.

JOE: Still diggin' up the roads Shay?

SHAY: I must've dug me way to Australia an' back Joe, d'yeh know that?

JOE: You're some man with a shovel alright. What about you Maurteen?

MAURTEEN: I'm on a site up in Highgate.

JOE: God, but there's good money to be made at the brick-layin' these days, what Maurteen?

MAURTEEN: Ah, dunno. It's a young man's game now Joe, have to be fit for price work.

JAP: Not at all! I'd lave ten youngfellas standin' at the gate at a days work.

JOE: An' what about yourself Jap? I'd say you're makin' a daycent shillin' too, hah?

JAP: Sure would I be still over here if I wasn't? Rakin' it in boy, rakin' it.

JOE: Lave it to yeh.

JAP: Oh yeah, foreman on a big site at Marble Arch, me. Have Git workin' with me too.

JOE: Foreman? Well jaysus lads, that's good goin'.

JAP: Twenty men under me Joe, English men too, not just Paddies. Darkies an' all.

JOE: Always said next step after bein' foreman is your own firm, that's the way I went.

JAP: Now yeh have it!

JOE: Start makin' money for yourself for a change.

JAP: The very words right out'a me mouth Joe.

SHAY: Your own gaffer...the only way.

JAP: Matter of fact Joe, wanted to talk to yeh 'bout that.

JOE: Talk?

JAP: Advice like. Ins an' outs a' startin' your own firm like.

JOE: Advice? For you?

JAP: Somethin' wrong with that?

JOE: No. I just –

JAP: There's nottin' in startin' your own firm Joe, nottin'! Just askin' for a few pointers, s'all.

JOE: I didn't mean it like that Jap.

JAP: See me an' Git, we've been thinkin' 'bout goin' out on our own, yeh know, back in Ireland.

JOE: You an' Git? Well fair play, fair play to yis. They say if yeh want to make money home's the place to go, alright. Anythin', anythin' I can do to help just call me.

JAP: I will, will.

(*GIT returns with a fresh bottle of whiskey and more sandwiches.*)

GIT: Bridie's ran out of ham. Corned beef and egg an' onion's is all that's left.

SHAY: So how did you get on out there?

GIT: Hah?

SHAY: You were out there that long that you must have thrown one into her.

JAP: That fella? No decent woman would touch him with a barge pole.

GIT: Would you get up the yard. Bar Shay and Maurteen's wives I've rode every woman in this town.

JAP: So between the two of us we've rode them all?

(*JAP laughs at his own joke.*)

SHAY: You wish fella, you wish.

JOE: Here Git. Jap was just tellin' me the news.

GIT: News...?

JAP: Was just tellin' Joe 'bout our plans.

GIT: Plans?

JAP: Yeah, just tellin' him.

(*GIT is lost but doesn't want to let JAP down.*)

GIT: You were? Oh grand, grand.

JOE: Out on your own, what?

JAP: Construction!

GIT: Construction!

JAP: Jaysus, but it's a great word that, must be a Paddy that cem up with that one.

MAURTEEN: An' guess what? If it all goes well I might just follow yis back.

GIT: You would?

MAURTEEN: In a flash lads, in a flash.

JAP: An' you'll be well looked after, wouldn't he Git?

GIT: Without a doubt.

MAURTEEN: Jobs for the boys, what?

JAP: Jobs me arse! Partners Maurteen, partners one an' all!

GIT: Are you serious Maurteen, you would…follow us back like?

MAURTEEN: Like a light.

GIT: An' what about the kids, school?

MAURTEEN: Aren't there schools in Ireland?

JAP: Best a' fuckin' schools!

MAURTEEN: Jaysus boys I'm tellin' yis, you get things goin' over there an' I'd be back in no time.

JAP: This time next year, this time next year everythin' should be up an' runnin'.

GIT: Yeah?

JAP: Easily.

(*GIT starts to get excited at the idea, spurred on by MAUR-TEEN's interest.*)

JOE: So where'll yis start up in Mayo or Dublin?

JAP: Oh jaysus, Dublin of course.

GIT: Dublin of course.

JAP: Sure what the fuck would you build in Mayo? This tiger bastard, want to get a piece of it before it's made extinct.

JOE: God, was over in Dublin a few weeks ago, jaysus, different city that it was. Christ I was walkin' around an' didn't know whether to go in for a pint or a pizza, true as God. Home. It's the place to be now alright, what?

SHAY: Home?

GIT: No place like it, as the fella ses.

SHAY: Home me bollox.

(*A short silence.*)

JAP: What ails you?

SHAY: Would yis ever stop all that shite talk about home an'
    cop on to yourselves?

JAP: Oh, he's off lads.

SHAY: This is our home. Here.

JAP: (*Teasing him.*) This room?

SHAY: You know well what I mean Jap. England.
    (*A beat.*)

JAP: I beg your pardon?

SHAY: Just sayin', here's home now, for all of us.

JAP: Would yeh listen to this fella lads.

SHAY: We've even been livin' here longer than we did in
    Ireland.

JAP: So.

SHAY: So.

JAP: Well that don't mean fuck all Shay.

SHAY: Course it does.

JAP: You tryin' to say that because I've been over here longer
    than I were in Ireland that I'm a Brit?

SHAY: More English than the English themselves.

JAP: Hey. Hey-fuckin'-hey, ain't no Brit me, ain't no fuckin'
    Hun.

SHAY: The shirt on your back, roof over your head?

JAP: Shirt on me back's from fuckin' China. Roof over me
    head's owned by a German.

SHAY: Just sayin', far as I'm concerned, here's me home, s'all.
    Have a nice little council flat, a dog, sure my kids'd be
    aliens back over there, aliens.

JAP: S'no country Shay, no country to rare kids in.

SHAY: Well it's a bit too fuckin' late for that now isn't it?

GIT: You made your bed…

SHAY: That's right. I made me bed an' it's better than any
    bed I left behind in fuckin' Ireland! A pigsty, that's what I
    left behind me, a fuckin' pigsty…all of us did.

JAP: So you here for good, that what you're sayin'?

SHAY: S'what I'm sayin' Jap, we all are.

JAP: Didn't you hear me just say I was goin' back?

SHAY: You're the same Maurteen. Stuck here too, you as well

Git.

GIT: Here, don't go writin' me off.

MAURTEEN: Or me nayther.

SHAY: Joe? You any plans to head back?

JOE: Not me. I'm here for good.

SHAY: See, we're all here and we're all goin' nowhere.

JAP: That's what you think fella, that's what you think.

SHAY: S'not what I think Jap, s'what I know.

(A pause. SHAY gets up and pours some more whiskey into his glass. MAURTEEN goes to the window and looks out.)

MAURTEEN: How much did that yoke set yeh back?

JOE: Ah come on now.

MAURTEEN: I'd say yeh could buy a house for what that car cost yeh.

JOE: A tax write off, yeh know yourself Maurteen.

MAURTEEN: A beauty.

JOE: Drivin' yourself?

MAURTEEN: I am alright.

JAP: The only thing he's drivin' is us up the wall.

JOE: Wanna try her out?

MAURTEEN: Hah?

JOE: Here, there's the keys, take her around the block for a spin.

JAP: And him full of drink? Leave that car where it is, one of us dead is enough for now.

(The sudden mention of death brings proceedings to a brief halt. The following is subdued. JAP pours a glass of whiskey.)

SHAY: We're runnin' low. Will I order another?

(JOE nods. SHAY goes to the door and calls.)

Bridie, another bottle of Powers when you're ready.

(JOE laughs to himself in an attempt to liven things up.)

JOE: D'yeh 'member lads, I say d'yeh 'member the time we were livin' in that kip in, where was it, Maida Vale?

GIT: Oh jaysus...! Kip is right.

MAURTEEN: An' that hungry pig that owned it.

GIT: A dirt bird.

JAP: Wouldn't mind but he was a Paddy too.

JOE: D'yous remember the time he cut the electricity off to try an' get us out?

SHAY: Thank God it was the Summer or we'd have froze to
    death.

JOE: Jackie Flavin…a gas man, he was workin' on a tunnel
    extension for the underground. 'Member…he brought
    these helmets home with him?

MAURTEEN: Them miners helmets, with the little lamp on
    the front? Jaysus I'd forgotten about them.

JOE: I'd stopped off to by some candles. I open the door an'
    what do I see? The boul Jackie an' Maurteen sittin' there
    with two of the helmets on readin' the paper. I'm standin'
    there yeh know, what the fuck, I'm thinkin' what's goin'
    on?

GIT: Jaysus they were great yokes. Used to be able to see
    yourself shave with them, shave an' shite.
    (*They all laugh at the memory of it.*)

JOE: They were some days, what?

JAP: We were mad bastards, what? Mad fuckers altogether!

JOE: There was some drinkin' done back then, what?

JAP: What d'yeh mean back then? Hasn't fuckin' stopped!
    What lads…still as mad as ever!

GIT: Here, here, 'member the night we were comin' out a'
    that place in Cricklewood? The Blue Duke?

JOE: Ohh…

JAP: Them Greek arsebandits?

MAURTEEN: Turks.

JAP: Greek fuckers.

MAURTEEN: Turks I'm tellin' yeh!

GIT: Greeks, Turks, who gives a shite? What I'm sayin' is oul
    Jackie took three a' them on on his own.

JAP: We weren't far behind.

GIT: Loafs one, loafs another then a kick into the balls to the
    other. Two seconds, all over in two seconds flat.

JAP: God what I'd give for them days again.

SHAY: Is your memory gone or what?

JAP: What now?

SHAY: What you'd give for them days! Jaysus, that's great
    that is, that's great altogether. Fuck sake, sardines man, we

were livin' like sardines. Two beds between six of us?

JAP: You were never able for the rough life you, poor mammy's boy. What did yeh expect you'd get when yeh cem, over a room in Buckingham palace?

SHAY: All I'm sayin' is they weren't the great days you're makin' them out for, s'all.

(*Beat.*)

They were tough, hard days. Grand, we were gettin' the ride, lots a' work, drink…but fuck lads, wasn't what we cem over for, was it?

GIT: Ah but it was good craic Shay, yeh can't deny that.

SHAY: Good craic? An' aren't we payin' for it now? Look at us, let everythin' pass us by. Instead of diggin' for gold the only diggin' we did was into some poor fuckers' stomach or the ends of our pockets for the price of a curer the next mornin'.

JOE: Sure what were we to know Shay, hah, straight off'a the farm, what were we to know?

SHAY: It's alright for you, you had sense, you broke loose an' look what happened to you.

JOE: Was just lucky, that's all.

SHAY: Would yeh go on out a' that. You saw the damage bein' done an' done the right thing.

JAP: The right thing? Right fuckin' thing? Come in one night an' tell us he's movin' out.

JOE: Hey…

JAP: Twelve months before we set eyes on yeh again.

JOE: Yeh know how it was lads…was workin' seven days a week, non stop. One week, Leeds, another Coventry.

JAP: Yeah. You could've even given us a shout. I'd've gone with you.

JOE: D'you hear this fella, back then you wouldn't get up off your arse to scratch it.

JAP: Next thing we know you've started up your own firm.

SHAY: We could've all done it too if we wanted to Jap, so don't be blamin' Joe, he wasn't responsible for us, no one was…not even ourselves.

(*A silence. GIT pours a glass of whiskey out.*)

GIT: Come on lads, come on… Are we forgettin' the day that's in it? To poor oul Jackie.

(*Raising his glass.*) Here's to you where ever yeh are.

(*They mumble a toast and drink some whiskey.*)

JOE: A terrible way to go lads, hah? A terrible end to so fine a man.

MAURTEEN: You know they couldn't even have the coffin opened he was that bad?

JOE: No...no, I didn't know that.

JAP: Sued, sued the bastards should be, for millions!

JOE: Any solicitor would take that case, I say any solicitor.

GIT: Yeah, well they'd be wastin' their time.

JAP: Hey.

GIT: Wastin' their time, yeh hear?

JAP: Hey fuckin' hey Gitna! Clear cut case, right?

GIT: Clear cut me hole.

(*GIT moves away and sits alone.*)

JAP: The platform was slippy, he lost his footin'.

GIT: I only told his father that so not to break his heart. An' even he didn't believe it.

JOE: Believe what?

JAP: He slipped, right?

JOE: What's all this about Git?

JAP: Nothin' Joe, don't be mindin' him.

JOE: Git?

MAURTEEN: Lave it be Joe.

JOE: No, no. Fuck it lads, there's somethin' goin' on.

JAP: Look can we stop all this death talk an' someone sing a song?

JOE: Steady on Jap.

(*A silence, JOE scans their faces for an answer.*)

What's this about Jackie not slippin' Git?

JAP: Can we not start this shite again. Shay, it's your turn to sing another, come on.

JOE: He'll sing in a minute!

(*A beat. JOE approaches GIT.*)

Now I asked a question. He did slip...didn't he?

JAP: Course he slipped!

JOE: Whist!

JAP: (*A little threateningly.*) Git...

(But GIT is having none of it.)

GIT: You wasn't there Jap, hear me, you wasn't there!

JAP: Doesn't matter whether I was there or not. I know Jackie Flavin an' that's not his form. That right Maurteen?

MAURTEEN: I dunno, I dunno at all.

JAP: Yeah, well I do an' I say he fuckin' slipped!

GIT: You can say it anyway yeh like Jap but I saw what happened an' that's that.

JAP: Maurteen, will yeh talk to this fucker!

MAURTEEN: Look the man was there Jap, what do I know?

JAP: He was there alright, full of drink. Easy to get things mixed up an' yeh full of drink.

GIT: Full of drink me bollix, I'd five pints on me, that's all.
(JAP looks over to the door.)

JAP: What's keepin' that whore with the drink?
(JOE's tone changes, the drink is making him a little aggressive.)

JOE: Fuck the drink, now is somebody gonna answer my fuckin' question or what?
(GIT looks at JAP then to JOE.)

GIT: He'd been in great form an' us playin 'pool in a boozer off Baker St, great form altogether. Then, I dunno, he started to get mopey.

JOE: Mopey?

GIT: You know, sad, maudlin' like.

JOE: Mopey? Maudlin'? What the fuck's he on about?

JAP: Shite, that's what!

GIT: It was the way he was for the last few months, wasn't he lads? Always down, depressed.

JAP: No more than the rest of us.

GIT: Yeah but…but not that way.

MAURTEEN: We should've done somethin'.

JAP: What? Done fuckin' what?

MAURTEEN: Should've helped, s'all I'm sayin'. Should've done somethin'.

JAP: How do yeh give a man help an' he not lookin' for any?
(GIT has moved across and is sitting alone.)

GIT: He was gettin' worse so we left that kip and went to

another one across the road.

(*JAP slams his glass down and gets up.*)

JAP: Agh that's it! That's fuckin' it, I'm goin'. Where's me
coat? Fucked if I'm listenin' to this shite again.

(*A silence.*)

JOE: Go on, Git.

GIT: We were only in there a few minutes when he started to
cry.

JAP: Shite! The man never cried a tear in his life.

GIT: Cry about his Ma, his Da an' some girl called Barbara.

JAP: Barbara! Barbara fuckin' who, hah, Barbara who?

JOE: (*Roaring at JAP.*) Can you shut your fuckin' mouth for a
minute!

(*A silence falls.*)

MAURTEEN: I remember her.

JAP: Well I don't.

JOE: Fuck sake you...!

MAURTEEN: He'd bin engaged to her for about a year when
he took the boat with us. Said he was only stayin' till he
had enough for the weddin'.

JAP: Never, never said nottin' to me 'bout no weddin'.

JOE: (*Roaring.*) Jap, I won't fuckin' tell yeh again!

(*A silence.*)

MAURTEEN: Seems she gev up on him after a few years an'
married someone else. He was out on a job in Brentford
one day when he hears someone callin' out his name. He
looks up from the trench to see this woman smilin' down
at him, her eyes beamin' as he put it. It was your wan,
Barbara. Seemed she'd been livin' over here a good while,
settled down like, kids an' all, with some fella from Tyrone.
They had a bit of a chat an' then said their goodbyes. Well
he started to dwell on it, yeh know, started to regret ever
commin' over, that he missed out on everythin', yeh know,
wife, kids an' all. An' it wasn't the normal way you'd get
depressed at Christmas or a Ma's birthday, this was like a
cloud, a big black cloud had took hold of him an' wouldn't
let go. He'd cry regular too, yeh know, often at the end of a
night's drinkin' we'd find him locked in the jacks cryin' like
a baby.

JOE: An' did yis not do anythin' for him?

GIT: Sure what could anyone do?

MAURTEEN: 'Twenty-five years', his last words to me an'
I lavin' 'Twenty-five years over here an' only a one room
flat in Hammersmith to show for it.'

JAP: Only! Only a one room flat? There's people'd cut off
their right arms for a one room flat, cut their arms off.

GIT: He didn't own the fuckin' place, did he?

JAP: Do you own a place? Do I own a place?

JOE: An' you let him go alone?

MAURTEEN: Git stayed with him. Me an' Jap headed off to
The Lion.

GIT: Jaysus, but he couldn't stop sobbin'. People were lookin'
at us. I was gettin' embarrassed like someone might think
we were two queers or somethin'. He finished his drink an'
said he was goin', I threw mine back an' said I'd walked
him to the tube station then join the lads. I dropped him
off an' was a bit up the way when I realised I'd no smokes
left with me so I turned back to ask him for one. I hopped
over the ticket machine an' went in after him. He was the
only one there. God, God he was still at it, only bawlin' this
time, he was cursin' too, cursin' England, cursin' Ireland,
cursin' everything that came into his head. I stood there
watchin' him, not knowin' what to say or do, when slowly I
felt the breeze a' the tube push out of the tunnel an' brush
across me face. He seemed to stop cryin' as the air blew
out an' looked into the tunnel...stared into it like. I could
hear the train gettin' louder as it approached, the wind
gettin' faster, colder. He walked over to the edge of the
platform like yeh do when your tube comes an' looked into
the tunnel, like...like there was someone in there. As the
lights of the train got brighter he wiped the tears from his
eyes, blessed himself an' walked straight out under it as it
came out from the tunnel. Walked straight off the platform
like he was about to walk on air.

(*A dead silence, JOE speaks quietly and blesses himself.*)

JOE: Jesus, Mary an' Joseph.

(*JAP is holding back the tears, he is under immense strain
in doing so.*)

JAP: No! No fuckin' way Gitna. No fuckin' way I said, d'yeh

54

hear me? Jackie Flavin wouldn't do a thing like that, he wouldn't.

SHAY: He did Jap…he did.

(*A pause.*)

GIT: Everything was all silent. The driver, God love him, he got out of his train not knowin' what to say or do. I stayed on as everyone was asked to leave so they could remove the body. Fuckin' hour, a full fuckin' hour it took.

(*GIT pauses, on the verge of tears, he succumbs.*)

They…they had to reverse it to get at him.

(*JOE goes and comforts GIT, throws an arm over his shoulder and leads him to a seat.*)

JAP: Christ will one a' yis see what's keepin' that cunt with the whiskey?

MAURTEEN: Hey, hey…take it easy, take it easy Jap.

SHAY: I'll get it, I'll get it, relax you.

(*SHAY gets up and exits.*)

GIT: I could've stopped him lads…all I had to do was go over to him an' he standin' there alone cryin' into the night.

(*A silence.*)

JAP: Told yeh not to open your mouth. Bollixed the whole day now, so yeh have.

GIT: Man asked a question, right? Man asked what happened.

JAP: Ruined the wake now, hope you're happy.

JOE: Arra come on lads, there's no need to be fallin' out with each other now, is there?

(*JAP picks up his coat and puts it on.*)

JAP: I'll see yis whenever.

MAURTEEN: For fuck sake!

JAP: What! What?

MAURTEEN: Sit down there like a good man an' don't be actin' the bollix.

JAP: The humour is off me now.

GIT: Lave him be.

(*JAP turns back.*)

JAP: Fuck you Gitna!

GIT: Fuck me? Hah, that's a good one, d'yeh hear that lads, fuck me!

JAP: Yeah fuck you an' fuck your walkin' on air shite.

GIT: Go on off to the flat an' sleep it off.

MAURTEEN: Would yeh do as I say an' take that coat off an' don't be actin' the bollix like a good man.

JAP: I sez lave me alone!

MAURTEEN: Look, whether Jackie did or didn't kill himself, it's no reason for us to be fallin' out, hah?

JAP: Like I get sad too Git, yeh know? I get depressed as well. God there's days I curse ever settin' foot over here. That mean I'm gonna jump under a train too?

GIT: Don't see what you're worried about, won't you be the one gettin' away from it all when you sail the high sea after Cheltenham?

JAP: That's right!

GIT: That's right!

JAP: An' I'll be goin' on me own too!

GIT: Great, didn't want to go with you anyway.

JAP: Sound.

GIT: Sound.

JAP: Can't wait the fuck to get away outta this kip an' away from yis all.

GIT: Good for you!

JAP: Yeah good for fuckin' me!

GIT: Right so...

JAP: Yeah, right so...!

(*A silence. JAP stands in a huff.*)

MAURTEEN: Will yous two ever shut up, yis are like two fuckin' oulwans.

(*MAURTEEN goes to JAP.*)

Now you take that coat off and don't be actin' the gobshite. (*MAURTEEN helps JAP take his coat off. A short silence as SHAY returns with a bottle of whiskey. He thrusts it at JAP.*)

SHAY: There! Are you okay?

(*But JAP sits in a sulk. SHAY puts the whiskey down.*)

GIT: How...how the fuck lads...how the fuck did this happen?

JAP: What are yeh shitin' about now?

GIT: Days I bang me head off'a the wall wonderin' what it was that brought us all over here in the first place. I can't remember anymore. There's this photo I have in the flat of us all in Piccadilly circus, 'bout, 'bout three-four weeks after we arrived. There's the six of us, standin' there like six fuckin' matadors, the best of clothes, creases in our slacks you could shave with an' the smiles, smiles from ear to ear. Where the fuck are them boys gone lads, hah? Where are them lads now?

MAURTEEN: Boys to men Git, you know the way it is, boys to men.

GIT: Boys to men me bollix! God curse the day we ever set foot in this kip of a country, God curse it! Why, hah… why London, what was it all about?

JOE: Everyone was doin' it.

GIT: I mean we were all young boys an' we gettin' off'a that boat in Holyhead, young boys. Look at us now, old fuckin' men, old fuckin' men.

SHAY: Well don't blame me. Wasn't my idea we stayed.

MAURTEEN: Two years…two years we said we'd come for.

JAP: I was waitin' on one of yous to go back.

MAURTEEN: Hah?

JAP: You know, waitin' for one a' yous to make the first move.

MAURTEEN: Waitin' on one of us?

JOE: I was waitin' on Jackie.

SHAY: I'd've gone as soon as any of yous went.

MAURTEEN: Yeh mean, yeh mean we've all been waitin' on each other to make the first move?

GIT: Well that's great news, I must say, great fuckin' news altogether!

MAURTEEN: Jaysus…don't say that lads.

JOE: Hey come on, s'not all that bad. Haven't you an' Shay got beautiful children out a' stayin' over here?

SHAY: Beautiful fuckin' grandchildren yeh mean!

JOE: Yeh don't mean-jaysus, he's goin' to be a grandfather lads!

JAP: He already is.

JOE.: Oh…

SHAY: Now the other little whore…seventeen's all she is, seventeen and she's up the pole for some fuckin' gob shite.

MAURTEEN: We should've gone to America. New York, remember, that was my idea. London you said Jap.

JAP: I never said London!

MAURTEEN: Yeh fuckin' did!

GIT: He's right. 'We'll go to London an' make our fortune', that's what yeh said, am I right Shay?

SHAY: The very words.

JAP: Never said London, said Manchester! Big fuckin' difference pal.

SHAY: Said if we went to America we'd be drafted and sent out to Viet-fuckin'-nam!

JAP: Dead right we would've.

SHAY: An' the war already over! Would yeh get up the fuckin' yard Jap!

MAURTEEN: We'd've done well in America boys.

GIT: The Big Apple.

JAP: Fuck you an' the Big apple.

GIT: Be millionaires by now I bet yeh.

JAP: It's easy sayin' that now, isn't it? Easy sayin' that now an' you sittin' on the fence.

GIT: I'm sittin' on no fence.

JAP: Been on it that long it has a track worn across the crack of your arse!

SHAY: Well where ever we'd have gone we'd've done better than we did here, that's for sure.

GIT: Fuck you Jap.

JAP: Fuck me? What d'yeh mean, fuck me?

GIT: Fuck you an' your streets a' gold.

JAP: Hey, hey-fuckin'-hey, that weren't me, that were a fuckin' song! A fuckin' song remember? Never told no one they'd find their fortune over here, no one.

SHAY: Yes yeh did. Said we'd be rich in six months.

JAP: Never said any such thing!

SHAY: I remember the day well. We'd been in Dublin three weeks when he comes in one evenin'. 'Fuck this Dublin lads, fuck this Dublin I know of a better place.'

JOE: I borryed two pounds off'a you Git for me fare over.

GIT: God I was terrified on the boat goin' over. Never been at sea in me life.

JOE: None of us had, boys, none of us had.

MAURTEEN: All the same, we fell onto our feet soon as we arrived, say one thing about London. Had a lot a' fun in it.

SHAY: Yeah, too much fun, it led us astray, an' before we
knew it we'd forgotten what we came for in the first place.
(*A pause. The men sip there drinks in silence. After a
moment GIT starts to sing quietly and slowly.*)
'Oh Mary this London's a wonderful sight.'

JAP: Fuck off!

GIT: 'For there's people here workin' by day an' by night.'

JAP: Fuck off I said Git!
(*MAURTEEN joins in.*)

MAURTEEN/GIT: 'They don't sow potatoes nor barley
nor wheat but there's tons of them diggin' for gold in the
street.'

JAP: Arra fuck the lot of yis!
(*JOE and SHAY join in, none out of tune, none out of
rhythm.*)

MAURTEEN/GIT/JOE/SHAY: 'At least when I asked them
that's what I was told, so I just took a hand at this diggin'
for gold. But for all that I found there I might as well be,
where the mountains of Mourne roll down to the sea.'
(*They stop, smile at each other. A silence, JOE wipes some
tears from his eyes.*)

JAP: Don't know what you're cryin' for, you found plenty a'
gold in the streets.

JOE: An' what...I'm supposed to feel guilty?

JAP: No Paddies...no Paddies workin' for him he ses. An' why
is that, hah? Cause yeh can't get them...are yeh blind man,
all that gold took away your eyesight? You never seen the
queues a' men on the Cricklewood Broadway at seven a'
clock in the mornin' all waitin' all quein' in the hope they'll
pick up a bit of work? It's not Scottish accents they have,
not French! A bollox yeh are, a lyin' bollox Joe!

GIT: I thought you were goin'?

JAP: You know it's true Git, you know the score. Man
wouldn't give yeh a job if his life depended on it.

JOE: An' why is that, hah...come on Jap, you're the man with
all the answers.
(*A beat. JOE gets up and goes to where JAP is sitting.*)
No Paddies workin' for me. Will I tell you why? Cause
they're not worth a wank! None of them.

JAP: Listen to him...listen to Paddy Englishman.

JOE: A bunch of no good, lazy drunken bastards that'd get yeh
thrown off more jobs. Jaysus Christ I'd be out a' business
in a week if I were to give any of them a job, be bankrupt.
I got where I am by bein' cute. Think I cem over here
to end up on the Kilburn High Road of a Saturday night
cryin' into me pint an' singin' a' home? Think that's what I
kissed me mother an' father goodbye for? My fuckin' hole!
I cem over here for one reason an' one reason only, same
reason we all cem over so don't go shitin' at me 'cause
yeh got lost somewhere along the journey, Jap, don't go
blamin' me, okay!

JAP: You could've took us up with yeh Joe, could've dragged
us out a' the gutter.

JOE: An' have meself sucked back into it tryin'? Go and fuck
yourself!

(*JOE gets his coat and puts it on.*)

MAURTEEN: Hey, hey Joe.

SHAY: What's the story Joe?

JOE: Good luck to yis boys.

SHAY: Ah come on Joe. You're after buyin' another bottle.

JOE: I'm sure it won't go to waste.

JAP: Let him go Shay...let him fuck off in his fancy car.

(*JOE turns and faces JAP.*)

JOE: You're a sad bastard Jap, d'yeh know that, a sad fuckin'
bastard. Think you're the big shot, the man we all look to
for answers...well them days are gone Mucker. Them days
are gone. God forgive me but I wish it was you that went
under that fuckin' train.

(*JOE heads to the door and leaves. JAP goes to the door
and shouts after him.*)

JAP: Go on, go on, fuck off, we don't need yeh. Stuff your firm
up your arse if yeh can get it past all the English cocks that
are up there! Yeh fat fuckin' bastard!

(*MAURTEEN heads out to the toilet.*)

MAURTEEN: Well that's great that is, I say that's great altogether now.

JAP: And fuck you too!

(*GIT starts to fix his shirt and gets his coat.*)
What are you up to?

GIT: What does it look like?

JAP: Sit down there you an' cop on! Isn't the fuckin' eegit after payin' for another bottle of whiskey?

(*JAP settles back down.*)

GIT: You've a big mouth, d'yeh know that? A big fuckin' mouth.

JAP: What?

GIT: There were no need to talk to Joe, like that.

JAP: Was just speakin' the truth, 's all.

GIT: That right? Like yeh were speakin' the truth about your sack full a' riches?

JAP: What's that supposed to mean?

GIT: Don't get me...don't get me goin' Jap.

JAP: If you've somethin' to say spit it out.

GIT: I would only there'd be that much it'd drown yeh!

(*GIT heads to the door.*)

SHAY: Where yeh goin', The Lion?

GIT: The Lion is it? Yis can stuff The Lion up your arses for I'm havin' none of it anymore.

SHAY: Here, what am I after doin'?

JAP: Don't mind the fucker Shay, let him go, we'll be well rid of the moanin' bastard. Go on, piss off and find yourself a whore!

GIT: You're a fuckin' eegit Jap, d'yeh know that? A big fuckin' thick Paddy. Think none of us don't know what's goin' on, think none of us can't see through all this shite?

JAP: What shite?

GIT: Know how I'm out here today, know where I got the money? Had to pawn me watch. Thirty pound's all I got, all I have in me pocket, all I have in the world right now! Ain't no big job in Marble Arch Shay, ain't no foreman's job or nayther.

JAP: Wanker, what would you know?

GIT: Fucked off it we were last week for workin' too slow. Man said we weren't up to it.

JAP: Hey you!

GIT: We've been scratchin' our arses the last week lookin' for work.

SHAY: That true Jap?

JAP: What, what? Never been let got from work before?

SHAY: If I have I've never hid it from anyone.

GIT: That mornin' we'd only started on a trench when the gaffer comes over to us. Said a one armed man would have dug more than the two of us put together.

JAP: He only used that as an excuse.

GIT: Worse fool me for goin' out on the drink with yeh the night before. I wanted to be fresh the next mornin', able to get stuck in but no, I let you talk me into goin' on the piss across the road and fuckin' everything up for me.

JAP: Agh what ails yeh, we'll get another start next week.

GIT: A start? Are you out of your head. Were not wanted anymore Jap...too old, we've been left out to graze.

JAP: Speak for yourself.

GIT: I get nowhere with you, know that, fuckin' nowhere. S'like havin' this big weight on me back goin' any place with you, always draggin' me down, holdin' me back.

JAP: Then yeh know what to do then, don't yeh! Cut lose!

GIT: Yeah, well that's what I'm doin'. You may look for some-one else to share the flat with yeh.

SHAY: Come on lads...fuck sake.

JAP: My prayers are answered!

GIT: More's the pity I didn't do it years ago.

JAP: Go on, shag off. I'll manage. But I'll tell yeh one thing, I'll tell yeh one thing, don't come lookin' for work off me when it all works out, don't knock on my door.

GIT: I won't.

(*GIT exits giving JAP the two finger salute.*)

JAP: Fuckin' eegit.

(*SHAY gets his coat and puts it on.*)

SHAY: Hang on Git... I'll be along with yeh.

JAP: Not you too?

SHAY: S'all right for you...single man. You can stay out all day an' not a word from no one.

JAP: Not able for the drink anymore, none a' yis.

(*SHAY stops at the door and turns back.*)

SHAY: Don't mind Gitna, he'll be alright in the mornin'.

JAP: S'not my fault Shay...s'not my fault any a' this happened.

SHAY: Forget about it Jap.

JAP: Was just the hand we were dealt, that's all, the hand we were dealt.

(*As SHAY heads out the door.*) See yeh in The Lion later on?

SHAY: Maybe…maybe.

(*An awkward pause.*)

(*SHAY exits. JAP lights a fag and looks around the empty room. JAP pours a glass of whiskey and eats a sandwich. After a moment MAURTEEN returns form the toilet. He sees JAP is alone.*)

MAURTEEN: Listen boys, I need to put me head down for a – hey…where's everyone?

JAP: Good oul Maurteen. You're one a' the best, know that, rock solid.

MAURTEEN: What's the story?

JAP: Sit down there beside me boy and don't mind them others, me an' you'll finish the day.

(*MAURTEEN goes to the window and looks out.*)

MAURTEEN: Didn't even say goodbye?

JAP: Here give us your glass.

MAURTEEN: Are they all gone up to The Lion?

JAP: Sit down here you and don't be mindin' them eegits, me an' you'll drink for Jackie.

MAURTEEN: Nah…

JAP: What?

MAURTEEN: Fuck it…I'll head off home for a kip an' I'll see yis later.

JAP: Ah jaysus Maurteen…don't you go now…don't you bail out on me too.

MAURTEEN: Need a rest, bit of a kip an' I'll be game ball Jap.

(*MAURTEEN starts to gather his clothes and put them on.*)

JAP: You go back now an' yeh know yeh won't be allowed back out.

(*MAURTEEN stops what he's doing. His tone changes, menacing.*)

MAURTEEN: Hah?

JAP: Be under lock and key for the rest of the day.

MAURTEEN: Listen here fella I can come an' go when

I like in my own house, hear that, come and go when I
like!

JAP: Hey…hey now, don't start that.

MAURTEEN: I'm the King in my gaff, got that Jap, King!

JAP: You don't go botherin' that woman, yeh hear me now?

MAURTEEN: Me that calls the shots, no one else. An' if she
as so much opens her mouth, opens her fuckin' mouth…or
looks crooked at me! Jaysus!

(MAURTEEN heads for the door, JAP goes after him.)

JAP: No messin' Maurteen, yeh hear, no fuckin' messin' with
that woman.

(As MAURTEEN leaves.)

MAURTEEN: English fuckin' bitch! She that kept me here,
she that got pregnant… I'll break her fuckin' neck!

*(JAP comes away from the door and, wearied by the day,
sinks alone into a seat.)*

JAP: Well Jackie boy, guess it's just you an' me fella, just you
an' me.

(He pours another glass of whiskey and drinks it back.)
(Almost inaudible.) Bastard…!

*(He rests his head in his hands. He starts to cry slowly
and builds up until his whole body opens up and envelopes
him in a river of tears. He sits bawling. After a moment
GIT returns to the door, he stops when he sees JAP. JAP
hears him, he gets up, wiping the tears away, as if they
were never there.)*

Ah-ha… Gitna me oul segosia. I knew yeh wouldn't lave me.

GIT: You okay?

JAP: Me? Sure I'm grand, grand. Come on, sit down there an'
have a drink.

GIT: Was the whiskey I cem back for.

JAP: The whiskey?

(GIT gets the whiskey and puts it into his pocket.)
Oh…

*(GIT makes his way to the door. JAP sits back down, GIT
turns and looks at him, they hold each others gaze.)*
Why…why did he have to go an' do it Git? Why did he
have to go an' kill himself?

GIT: Don't be lookin' for any answers off'a me Jap.

(*JAP gets up and walks towards GIT.*)

JAP: Jaysus, things weren't great but we got by, an' so what if we never made it, so what if we never struck gold, hadn't we each other?

(*Suddenly JAP grips GIT's shoulders.*)

Get me outta this fuckin' country Git, get me out of it an' away back home!

GIT: Jap...

JAP: Yeh have to help me Git, yeh have to get me home.

GIT: The blind leadin' the blind yeh want, is it?

JAP: I don't know where I am anymore, who I am. All I see of meself is an old man lost. I just...just want to go home, Git, home.

GIT: Like yeh said yourself Jap, travel shop five minutes up the road.

JAP: Yeh know quite well I haven't the price of a stamp never mind the fair back.

GIT: You're some tulip, know that? Maybe, maybe me an' the boys can chip in an' get yeh a ticket?

JAP: Nah...can't return like this Git, can't.

GIT: Course yeh can.

JAP: Twenty-five years, twenty-five years an' what have I got to show for it, hah? I'd be a laughing stock.

GIT: There's no one gonna sit in judgement of yeh.

JAP: I'm vanishin' over here, the invisible fuckin' man.

I was someone at home, know that?

GIT: Sure weren't we all once upon a time, hah?

JAP: I'd a queue a' women lined up all waitin' for me to return home an' marry one a' them.

GIT: Yeh weren't the only one.

JAP: Wasn't no ordinary man, me. A force of nature! That's what I was. A force of fuckin' nature. I could dig trenches ten foot deep with me bare hands, rip up cobbled streets, an' with a sledge hammer, with a ten pound sledge I could lay a red brick building flat in five minutes! That was me, that was Jap Kavanagh.

GIT: An' you'll still do it, boy.

(*JAP looks at GIT, his tone changes.*)

JAP: Then you're a bigger fuckin' thick than me if yeh believe that.

(GIT looks at him, he smiles slightly.)

GIT: Are you gonna stay here on your own or what?

(JAP smiles at him then goes to the mirror and fixes himself up.)

JAP: We could've done it Git, could've been kings over hear, royalty an' all the good looks we had comin' over

GIT: Suppose, suppose nottin' lasts forever Jap, nottin', that's what me mother used to say anyway.

JAP: Looks like she was right.

GIT: Start again in the mornin' Jap, what? We'll start off from scratch an' have one more go.

JAP: Arra...

GIT: We'll knock the drink on the head, save like fuck till we've enough to show our faces back home and start all over?

JAP: You're sayin' that now an' we full 'a drink, but don't yeh know it'll be a different story entirely in the mornin' an' the drink gone?

GIT: Sure what if it is? Can't we get drunk all over again?

(JAP finishes off his glass.)

JAP: Right, come on an' we go.

GIT: Go? And where is it we'll go in this state Jap?

JAP: Sure where else but home Gitna? Where else but home?

(JAP puts his arm over GIT's shoulder as they head out the door together. The lights fade.)

The End.

BROTHERS OF THE BRUSH

For Mary and Chloe

Characters

LAR
aged thirty

HENO
aged thirty

JACK
aged sixty

MARTIN
aged forty

Brothers of the Brush was first produced by the Abbey Theatre, Dublin as part of the Peacock New Plays Series '93. It won the Dublin Theatre Festival 'Best New Play' award, and the Stewart Parker Award. The first performance took place on 7 October 1993 with the following cast:

LAR, Eanna Macliam

HENO, Liam Carney

JACK, Des Nealon

MARTIN, Johnny Murphy

Director, David Byrne

Designer, Paul McCauley

Lighting designer, Tony Wakefield

Stage directors, Colette Morris, Micil Ryan

Assistant director, Teresa Kane

ACT ONE

Scene 1

Mid-day, late November. Sunlight shines through the dirty panes of a window to light up the interior of a basement in an old house in the city. Paint tins etc. are grouped in a corner. A door on some chairs serves as a table, on which cups, old milk cartons and old newspapers are piled.

HENO is silently prowling around with a lump hammer. He tiptoes, about to let the hammer fly at the first thing that moves. The door opens. LAR enters carrying some floor boards. HENO jumps round and almost hits LAR with the hammer.

LAR: For jaysus sake!

HENO: Shh! (*He continues prowling.*)

LAR: What's wrong?

HENO: Keep still!

LAR: What is it?

HENO: Will you keep quiet! (*Prowls.*) Come out now… Let's see you ate this you black pig.

LAR: (*Picks up a brush.*) Who is it?

    (*LAR begins to prowl with HENO.*)

HENO: Let's see him take a lump out of this!

LAR: Who!

HENO: The bastarding rat that took a lump out of me lunch!

LAR: A rat! For jaysus sake! (*Throws brush down and walks over to where he is fixing the floor.*)

HENO: Two pounds that ham cost, two pounds! and I didn't even get a sniff of it! (*Looks around.*) Well I'll give it ham when I catch it… I'll shove a gallon of paint remover up it's arse!

LAR: What would mice want with your lunch?

HENO: Mice! There was rat down here a while ago as big as a Rottweiler! Big black eyes on the bastard! He was sitting on the table milling into me lunch. It looked me straight in the eyes as if to say: 'you come one step nearer and I'll eat you when I'm finished these.'

(*Walks around waving hammer.*)

Well let him try and take a lump out of this!

LAR: There's no rats down here, it's too damp for them.

HENO: I know that, you know that…but that bastard. I'll smash every tooth in his head.

LAR: Was probably a cat. Jack might've left the door open upstairs and it strayed in.

HENO: D'you think I'm blind? It was a rat I'm telling you.

LAR: I think you're going mad.

HENO: We must be all mad to stay working in this kip!

(*HENO has his back to LAR. LAR throws something at him. HENO jumps.*)

You bastard!

LAR: Come on Heno…if Kavanagh catches you.

HENO: (*Sits down.*) I'll tell you this. I'll not starve today. Kavanagh can go out and buy me me lunch.

LAR: Come on and give us a hand with these floorboards.

HENO: I will in me…

LAR: It won't take ten minutes.

HENO: I don't care if it takes ten seconds.

LAR: Once these are down that's the floor finished.

HENO: A carpenter now, are you?

LAR: Give us over the saw.

HENO: What'll you be doing next for him…putting a few slates on the roof?

(*Goes and gets the saw himself. Lays a plank of wood across a chair.*)

LAR: Hold onto the end of this till I cut it.

HENO: I won't hold on to as much as a nail. That's a job for a chippy.

LAR: All I'm doing is banging a few bits of wood down.

HENO: Once you start that it's goodnight. He'll have us up to all different jobs.

LAR: Are you going to help me?

HENO: I'm not a builder's labourer and neither are you.

LAR: Here we go again.

HENO: *Amo, Honorous, Obitium.*

LAR: What's that…the favourite in the three-thirty?

HENO: You don't even know the motto!

LAR: 'Where's me wages?' That's the only motto I know or care about!

HENO: Love, Honour and Obedience.

LAR: You can have them for your lunch, see how well they'll fill you.

HENO: You're a tradesman, Lar, a skilled worker.

LAR: There's only one skill Heno. (*Taps his pocket.*) Fill that up every Friday with as much as you can. Once you've mastered that you're on the pig's back.

HENO: The only one in here on the pig's back is Kavanagh. One pig on top of another. (*Puts down the hammer and gets back to working.*) I don't suppose you've the price of a ham roll till I get me labour?

LAR: Haven't a tosser.

HENO: No, you never do, do you?

LAR: Where's that fortune you made in London?

HENO: I'm back nine months! Money doesn't last forever you know.

LAR: You stop all your drinking and it wouldn't be long before you had a nice lump sum put away.

HENO: Would you listen to yourself!

LAR: That's how I've me own house.

HENO: Did you get too good for the flats?

LAR: I decided to move out when a child in a pram asked me for a light.

HENO: All lace curtains and cushions, huh?

LAR: Best thing that ever happened to me.

HENO: And I bet you've a little dog, a little poodle called Curly or something?

LAR: Great big garden too. Roses out the front and tulips out the back.

HENO: It's far from roses you were rared. Cabbages and piss-in-the-beds more like it!
(*Pause. LAR starts hammering some nails down.*)
There's no way I'd rent a flat in here…someone'll kill themselves on that floor.

LAR: This one is rented out already. They're moving in on Monday. Flats! That's where the money is nowdays.

HENO: Kavanagh says your man's places all over the city. Buys buildings ready to collapse, does them up and rents them out.

LAR: More luck to him once he gets Kavanagh to do them up.

HENO: Anything that was good in the kip was ripped out and is now in the window of every antique shop in Francis St... all that's left is a shell.

LAR: Once things look alright on the outside you can get away with anything.

HENO: You can't tear all the good bits out and expect it to stay the same.

LAR: Well if it does come tumbling down we won't be here. (*LAR hits his finger with the hammer.*)

HENO: Serves you right!

(*Pause.*)

Here, it's worth over a million tonight.

LAR: What is?

HENO: The lotto.

LAR: I suppose you've your numbers done.

HENO: Course I have. Three pounds worth on a Wednesday and a fiver on Saturday, a tenner sometimes if I do alright on the horses.

LAR: Every week?

HENO: Yeah.

LAR: Ever win?

HENO: Does it look like it?

LAR: A waste of good money.

HENO: You should loosen up Lar... Come out on the tear with us some time, like the old days.

LAR: Piss all me money away?

HENO: You never spend a penny on yourself nowdays.

LAR: It's hard enough making it.

HENO: And what's it for but to spend?

LAR: And do you ever *spend* a night in at home?

HENO: I'd rather sit in here with them rats! (*Stops working.*) Between *Home and Away, Neighbours, Emmerdale* bleedin' *Farm*! I don't know whether I'm coming or going. And if they don't do me head in she does. If it's not money she does be moaning about it's the state of the place, fix this, fix that. It's not my fault if I do be too tired to do a bit of

74

work when I get home. And what does she be doing all day, huh? What's she doing while I'm out trying to make a living? I'll tell you, she sits in front of the telly on her fat arse eating banana sandwiches and drinking tea while I'm stuck in here freezing to death, surrounded by a plague of fuckin' rats feasting themselves on my poxy lunch!

LAR: You made your bed.

HENO: I'm not the one with the mortgage. I'll be sitting on a high stool waiting for me six numbers.

LAR: You'll be waiting a long time.

HENO: I wouldn't tell a soul if I won.

LAR: You'd soon move out of the flats then.

HENO: I would not. I crown meself king of them.

LAR: Run off and buy yourself a mansion in Howth.

HENO: I'd give her and the kids a few grand, shag off on the piss and never lift a finger for the rest of me life.

LAR: If I won, I'd pay the bank what I owe them and then take the family all over the world… To America, always wanted to see the Grand Canyon, always wanted to stand on the edge and let a big 'Yahoo!' into it.

HENO: I know the yahoo I'd let, you'd be able to hear it on the moon, never mind the Grand Canyon.

LAR: Then I'd open a shop, nothing fancy, just a small one on a corner, cigarettes, newspapers, that kind of thing. I'd pack the kids off to college and take it easy.

HENO: A boozer, that's what I'd buy! *Heno's* I'd have written across the front. All pints a pound! Opening hours: when ever you feel like it! Closing time…when ever you feel like it!

LAR: I'd get a jag too…a big red one.

HENO: There'd be a betting shop at one end of the bar and a chipper at the other. The only time you'd need leave was to sign on or go to bed. But the very first thing I'd do… I'd call a taxi and get it to drop outside. I'd come in and sit down on this chair here and wait till Kavanagh came… I'd let him start roaring and shouting about me getting up to do a bit of work. 'Kavanagh', I'd say, wouldn't even call him Martin, 'Kavanagh, see that paint brush? Well you can go and shove it up the high hole of your arse!'

(*They laugh.*)

LAR: Suppose there's no harm dreaming.

HENO: Dreaming? There's no dreaming. All you need is six numbers. Here, we could do a syndicate, me, you and Jack, a fiver each.

LAR: Jack part with a fiver!

HENO: Over a half a million each we'd pick up!

LAR: Meanwhile, back on planet earth, the men get on with their daily chores!

(*LAR starts working again. HENO looks at him.*)

HENO: I remember the day you'd down tools if you saw someone doing the likes of that!

LAR: Five minutes work, that's all.

HENO: You'd've had a carpenter sent for or the job stopped.

LAR: The chances I took.

HENO: Chances? You were right...any messing and all out!

LAR: For all the good it did us.

HENO: And now look at you.

LAR: Them were the days.

HENO: Were?

LAR: Are you the same man you were four years ago?

HENO: Apart from the odd grey hair.

(*Pause. He takes a kettle from the table and empties it.*)

LAR: It's only a quarter past twelve.

HENO: He won't be here for ages. Bet you he's still in bed after another night on the town.

LAR: He could walk in that door any minute. And if he feels that kettle warm...

HENO: Spends in a night what he gives us a week!

LAR: It's his money.

HENO: That he got for what? It's us that does all the work.

LAR: Would you rather we'd none to do?

(*LAR exits and is heard filling the kettle. He returns and plugs it in. He looks out a window.*)

HENO: Looks like it's going to snow.

LAR: I suppose you've money down for a white Christmas?

HENO: Wouldn't like to be dead down here if we do. You could be dead down here and no one would notice.

LAR: Are you looking forward to it?

HENO: Snow?

LAR: Christmas!

HENO: It's only a headache.

LAR: This'll be me first Christmas working in two years...
Won't know meself with the few bob, be able to get the
kids whatever they want.

HENO: Never mind the kids, an oul van is all I want. If I'd a
van I'd go out on me own.

LAR: I heard that before.

HENO: Good work. That's all you need, good work'll give
you a good name, a good name and you'll never be idle.

LAR: There's too many out there with oul vans that's what has
the game the way it is, they have us at each others throats
for work.

HENO: I could make a fortune.

LAR: It's too late now.

HENO: I'm only thirty.

LAR: With five kids?

HENO: Should've made me move years ago.

LAR: Well...we had our chance?

HENO: (*Looks at LAR.*) Did you last long with that builder?
(*LAR ignores him and starts working again.*)
You should've followed me.

LAR: I'll have this floor safe and sound in no time.

HENO: Did you make anything out of him?

LAR: Give us over them nails.

HENO: Bet you didn't make a penny.

LAR: Heno...that bag of nails!

HENO: How much?

LAR: Heno! Them ones there.

HENO: A few ton?

LAR: Will you give us over the jaysus nails!

HENO: Bet it's all in the bank.
(*LAR gets up and gets nails himself.*)

LAR: That's how I own me own home.

HENO: It's not yours, the bank owns it.

LAR: I put two thousand cash into it meself.

HENO: Two thousand! I drank that an' I in London!

LAR: And why didn't you stay there?

HENO: You wouldn't be working if I did.

LAR: Was only a rough patch I was going through.

(*The sound of some planks falling against a scaffold. They run to the window and look out.*)

HENO: Look at that poor bastard out there. Shouldn't even be painting in this weather.

LAR: He's well wrapped up.

HENO: The state of the scaffold! You'd want to be a stunt man to work on this job.

LAR: No one's come to any trouble, touch wood.

HENO: It's a miracle no one broke their legs. It's like an assault course trying to work in here with all them floor-boards missing. But there's more than that floor in here that needs fixing.

LAR: Do you ever shut up?

HENO: I could turn this shop into a proper operation.

LAR: Heno! Don't start.

HENO: (*Points out.*) If he falls off that thing he's a goner, the same for any of us working in here. It's handy work getting the dole but what use is that if we're not insured?

LAR: All the more reason for me to get this floor fixed!

(*The sound of a door upstairs being closed. They wait till they recognise the sound of the footsteps.*)

HENO: Jack.

(*JACK enters. He is wearing a thick heavy coat, a scarf and boots. He is caked in old paint. He hobbles over to a chair and sits. He lifts the steaming kettle and sits it on his lap, with the steam he heats his fingers.*)

That you falling out there?

JACK: Bastarding yoke!

LAR: Off the scaffold?

JACK: Scaffold? It's worse than a gallows! You need a poxy ice pick to work on the jaysus thing!

HENO: You didn't fall off the top, did you?

JACK: Would I be sitting here if I did?

HENO: Claim off the bastard!

LAR: Where did you fall from?

(*JACK mutters a reply.*)

Where?

JACK: The bottom!

LAR: (*Laughs.*) How do you fall off the bottom of a scaffold?

JACK: May as well've broken me neck.

LAR: He just wants to come in out of the cold.

JACK: One of yous should be working out there.

HENO: (*Takes the kettle off him.*) That's for the tea.

JACK: Never mind the tea… I have to thaw out! (*Blows into his hands.*) Would it be alright to light a fire in here?

LAR: And burn the kip down?

JACK: Just a little one in a paint tin!

HENO: A good hot drop of rosie is what you want.

JACK: I don't know what I'd do without me hot water bottle. (*Takes a bottle of water from his coat pocket. Sees HENO's lunch on the floor. Picks it up.*) Don't tell me they were at it again?

HENO: For the last time!

JACK: Bastard mice, you can't leave a thing down!

HENO: Rats! Rats I'm telling you…that big!

JACK: Poison's the man for them.

HENO: Poison? That bastard eats poison for his breakfast!

JACK: I thought he said he was going to get a few traps?

HENO: Like he said he was going to get the toilets fixed!

JACK: (*Opens a sandwich.*) Nice bit of ham there.

HENO: Picnic bleedin' ham! Me favourite.

LAR: Picnic is right!

JACK: They weren't all ruined, where they?

HENO: What?

JACK: (*Sniffs them.*) Smell alright to me.

HENO: Of course they smell alright, they were fresh!

JACK: (*Bites one.*) Taste alright.

LAR: Jaysus Jack!

HENO: There was a rat's fat arse all over them!

JACK: Tell your mot she makes a lovely sambo.

HENO: When you're finished them you can go and clear them toilets out by shoving your head down the bowl!

LAR: All in there needs is a few kettles of boiling water.

HENO: The last man that had a crap in there was Daniel O'Connell!

JACK: (*Laughs.*) I should write that on the plaque outside: Daniel O'Connell crapped here!

LAR: They're only blocked I'm telling you.

HENO: Well I'm not doing it! That's a plumber's job, or do you fancy yourself as one of them too? There should've been a builder in here on this job. We should've been able to march in when they had the job finished and then got down to work.

JACK: Kavanagh hire a builder! Are you mad?

HENO: He expects us to do it all!

JACK: If he hears you moaning like that he'll send you packing! (*Gets up and hobbles around.*) Jaysus, I'm bursting for a crap!

HENO: Run across and use the pub.

JACK: Can't.

HENO: Why not?

JACK: We're barred, the lot of us…said we're not to go near them again.

HENO: Did he now?

JACK: Roared it at the top of his voice.

LAR: What do you expect in them rags?

JACK: I'm going to have to use that kip in there!

HENO: You're taking your life into your hands if you do.

JACK: Jaysus I hate this kip! Should be at home in me bed snoring me head off.

LAR: Sure you do that in here.

JACK: Probably won't get to retire… Die on the job, that'd be my luck.

LAR: Five more years Jack, that's all you've left. You'll be drawing your pension while we're stuck in holes like this!

HENO: Yeah, you lucky bastard. You won't have to leap out of bed on icy mornings like these. Can stay in bed all day and then ramble across the road to your local.

JACK: For what, a glass of water? You don't think you get that much money on the pension.

LAR: I'd say you've a nice little nest egg put by.

JACK: (*Goes over to toilet.*) Should've got out of this game years ago, should've moved on…started me own little firm.

(JACK exits to toilet.)

HENO: Look at that! Into that stinking smelly pit and it doesn't even bother him.

LAR: You shouldn't be saying too much in front of him, it all goes back to Martin.

HENO: And where'll you go to the toilet now?

LAR: It's lunch time, you don't expect them to let him waltz into a pub in them rags?

HENO: We're after being barred.

LAR: Then we'll find somewhere else.

HENO: What do we do for the rest of the day...carry a paint pot around with us?

LAR: That's not a bad idea.

HENO: I wouldn't put that past you either.

LAR: Yak-yak-yak.

HENO: I'll not be reduced to this for the rest of me days. D'you know how much he's getting for this job, do you? Five and a half thousand! Jack told me. All cash...won't have to pay a penny tax.

LAR: Once he gets cash we get cash.

HENO: And d'you know when he took you on he was going to pay you less than me. Told me to tell you I was on twenty-five a day.

LAR: Would still've took it. Was starting to think that I'd never work again, that I'd spend the rest of me days sitting in front of the telly with the remote control stuck in me hand. *(Pause.)*
I watched the whole of the Gulf war, then went out to sign on one day and missed the bleedin' ending!

(JACK returns. He goes over to pick up an empty paint tin.)

JACK: There's no way I'm using in there, I heard something move!

HENO: What are you doing with that?

JACK: I have to go somewhere.

HENO: *(Grabs tin off him.)* You have another thing coming if you think you're going to start that lark in here!

JACK: *(Grabs tin back.)* Well I can't hold it in, can I!

HENO: Go out into the yard!

JACK: And have the Khyber pass frozen off me...get out of

the way before I do it in here! (*Walks to door.*)

HENO: You dirty oul bastard you!

(*Pause.*)

What am I doing here, what am I doing surrounded by rats, filth and dirt birds!

LAR: A man's gotta do what a man's gotta do.

HENO: I mean I got up out of a warm bed and paid a bus driver to take me here.

LAR: Your rat'll have something else to chew on.

HENO: I don't find it funny.

LAR: Have you never done that before?

HENO: Are you sick in the head? A muck savage wouldn't carry on like that!

(*LAR Laughs.*)

Go on, laugh, make a joke out of it like everything else.

LAR: There'll be a white ring around his arse.

HENO: He'll have the whole kip smelling of it now. (*Shouts.*) I hope you poisoned yourself on them sandwiches! (*Tries to open a window. It won't budge.*) Give me a hand with this before we're all fumigated.

LAR: It's nailed shut.

HENO: I must be losing the bit that I have putting up with all this.

LAR: Just get your head down and get on with it like the rest of us.

HENO: I'm having withdrawal symptoms...need a dose of reality in me life. (*Looks out window.*) If there's any reality still out there.

(*HENO sees the kettle is boiling he unplugs it and makes some tea. After a while JACK returns buttoning up his overalls.*)

JACK: Let your rat take a lump out of that and see how far he gets.

HENO: I hope you didn't leave it out there in the hall.

JACK: I put it in your pocket! (*Sits down.*) It's getting worse out too. One of yous'll have to work outside for a while.

HENO: Not me!

JACK: A jaysus wino went by this morning and asked me if

I wanted the loan of an overcoat. Told me the Vincent de Paul were giving them out up the road. Go on…one of yous go out for a change, give us a chance of working in here in the warm.

HENO: In here…warm?

LAR: Have you not got a pair of gloves with you?

HENO: How is he supposed to paint with gloves on?

LAR: Don't worry Jack, this time next week.

JACK: If I last that long.

HENO: There's nothing definite yet.

LAR: Jack said there's enough work in it to keep us going right up to March.

JACK: End of March at least.

LAR: D'you hear that Heno…the end of March!

HENO: I'll believe it when I see it.

LAR: We'll have a mountain of work.

JACK: There's a lovely canteen in it too. You can get a fry in the mornings for a pound, a pound! And as much toast as you like.

HENO: Any carpentry for St Joseph there?

LAR: (*Sings.*) 'I'm dreaming of a busy Christmas…'

JACK: (*Stuffing his mouth.*) He'll be needing a charge hand.

HENO: What?

JACK: A foreman.

HENO: For three painters?

JACK: He'll need more than us Heno. Wait'll you see the size of the place.

HENO: He doesn't pay anyone the proper rate so he's hardly going to pay anyone to run the job.

JACK: Not at all. He pays a pound extra on the hour to whoever has the shout.

(*JACK rubs his hands and winks.*)

HENO: One fifty an hour's the proper rate.

JACK: Well it's good enough for me boys.

HENO: What do you mean?

JACK: I'm getting the shout.

(*Pause.*)

Did I say something wrong?

LAR: More luck to you.

JACK: And there's more... Big day for me today lads.

HENO: Having your monthly bath?

JACK: I've a nice few bob coming in.

HENO: (*Sits beside him.*) Get a tip for the horses?

JACK: Getting a loan.

HENO: (*Gets back up.*) Who'd give you a loan?

JACK: I'm getting seven hundred pounds.

HENO: Seven hundred pence, more like it!

JACK: She put in for a credit union loan a while back. She
    collects it today.

HENO: What are you going to do with seven ton?

JACK: I know what I'd love to do with it.

HENO: I'd say you do.

JACK: She wants the gaff done up, getting a bit of carpet, a
    new fridge, few things like that.

HENO: You'll want more than seven.

JACK: Twenty-five quid a week is all we have to pay back.

HENO: How will you spare twenty-five quid a week?

JACK: Won't I be getting the foreman's rate?

    (*The sound of a door shutting upstairs. JACK runs into
    the toilet, the others jump up and start painting. HENO
    climbs up a ladder and paints the wrong colour on the
    wall. MARTIN enters. He sniffs the air.*)

MARTIN: What's that smell? (*Looks up at HENO.*) Are you
    colour blind?

HENO: I took up the wrong pot.

MARTIN: (*Realises that HENO's just got back to work. Goes to
    table to feel tea pot.*) One o' clock boy, one o' clock you have
    your tea! (*Calls.*) Jack! Get out here. (*No answer.*) Why isn't
    Jack out there? (*Silence.*) Where is he? (*Calls again.*) Jack...
    get out here I said!

JACK: (*Returns.*) I just came in to get a heat...me hands were
    gone numb.

MARTIN: Get back out and finish them railings!

JACK: That scaffold's dodgy, I slipped off it.

MARTIN: You stupid eegit, can you not look where you're
    going?

JACK: It shakes all the time and the planks are frosted.

MARTIN: I don't think you're able for the work any more.

HENO: You try and work on it for five minutes!

MARTIN: Who's talking to you!

HENO: We nearly had a corpse on our hands this morning.

MARTIN: (*Laughs.*) We'll have to get him put down...what lads?

LAR: Sell him off to the knackers to make glue.

JACK: It's not fair Martin. We should all have turns working out there.

MARTIN: Agh shut up and don't be annoying me! Me head's splitting, didn't get to bed till three this morning.

HENO: Isn't it well for you?

MARTIN: Are we on target? (*No reply.*) I said are we nearly finished?

JACK: Don't look at me.

MARTIN: Is the top floor done?

LAR: I second coated it this morning.

MARTIN: It's not even glossed yet? Jaysus...what about the second floor?

HENO: The ceiling needed another coat.

MARTIN: Jaysus Heno!

HENO: I can't help it if the paint won't cover. Will I give it a fifty-fifty?

MARTIN: No! It's only down for two. If it won't cover leave it for her to see, if she wants another coat she'll have to pay extra.

HENO: I thought –

MARTIN: And the windows?

HENO: There's a lot of work in them sashes.

MARTIN: Come on lads! Get the finger out, this job is running two days over.

HENO: That's your fault for pricing it arseways.

MARTIN: It better be done by tomorrow.

HENO: There's a lot of work in this place, you don't realise it.

MARTIN: I priced this job to be done in five weeks.

HENO: We need more paint anyway.

MARTIN: More!!! But I only left two gallons here the other

day.

LAR: Some of the walls needed another coat.

MARTIN: Two is all they get! One if I can get away with it.

HENO: It's watered down too much.

MARTIN: Well I don't mix it. You're supposed to be the tradesmen… If you can't use the paint then get lost. It's costing me too much money this job.

HENO: Not as much as staying out till three in the morning.

MARTIN: If you moved your brush as fast as your tongue we might be out of here on time.

JACK: If we didn't have to keep marching across to the pub to use the jax!

HENO: And we can't use that any more…we've been barred.

MARTIN: (*Laughs.*) Barred…from a jax?

JACK: Where are we supposed to go now?

MARTIN: Serves you right for drinking so much tea.

HENO: And my lunch was destroyed again this morning!

MARTIN: Sure it was only bread and butter.

HENO: Bleedin' ham, that's what it was! And I want the money off you for it!

MARTIN: Get up the yard!

HENO: You can give me the money for a roll.

MARTIN: You want me to feed you as well as pay you?

HENO: I have nothing for me lunch… I'm starving.

MARTIN: How much is a roll?

HENO: One fifty.

MARTIN: One fifty? Jesus that's where the money is nowdays. (*Puts his hand into his pocket takes out some coins.*) There…one fifty, go out and get me a roll! (*Laughs.*)

HENO: Very funny!

MARTIN: You shouldn't leave your lunch lying around.

HENO: You're supposed to get traps.

MARTIN: As if I'd nothing else to do! It'd be a different story if I said I'd no work, that I lost a job while I was out buying mouse traps.

HENO: (*Looks for support from the others. He doesn't get it.*)

LAR: (*Breaks silence.*) Well…what's the story…on the factory?

MARTIN: I've just come from there. Had a meeting with the manager, Mr Rodgers.

HENO: (*Mocking.*) Mr Rodgers…

JACK: It's on?

MARTIN: I'm going to need a few painters.

JACK: Will I tell Trevor to come in?

MARTIN: Don't be annoying me.

JACK: A bit of work for the Christmas.

MARTIN: Who am I… Santy Claus?

JACK: Ah come on Martin…your cousin!

MARTIN: (*Ignores JACK. Goes over to the wall HENO is working on.*) Is that stuff going on alright?

HENO: Not a bother.

MARTIN: Have you enough?

HENO: Plenty.

MARTIN: What ever's left keep it. You wouldn't believe how much that cost.

HENO: Here… I mightn't be in in the morning.

MARTIN: What!

HENO: I'll be off collecting me big lotto cheque, over a million tonight.

MARTIN: What would you get for a million nowdays?

HENO: A lot more than I'd get for this cheque you gave me for overtime last week. Bounced in every pub I tried to cash it in.

MARTIN: Did you ever hear of a bank?

LAR: If he went into a bank they'd think he was there to rob it.

HENO: Come on…give us the money for it. (*Gives MARTIN the cheque.*)

MARTIN: I've no cash on me now. I'll sort you out tomorrow when I'm doing the wages. (*Goes to put cheque in his pocket.*)

HENO: I'll hold onto that, thank you. (*Takes cheque.*)

MARTIN: So…we'll be out of here the weekend?

JACK: I can't work fast on that thing, have to hold on with one hand to keep steady.

MARTIN: Yes or no!

JACK: I'm not the only one here.

MARTIN: It better be, or else you'll be in on a ghoster and Saturday and Sunday.

HENO: Count me out for Sunday.

MARTIN: You heard me say we've got to be out of here.

HENO: If you spent as much time here as you do in the night clubs we might be nearly finished on time. Paint brushes don't bite you know!

MARTIN: I know, and I employ you to use them!

HENO: Well I won't be in, it isn't worth me while.

MARTIN: If you're not in you needn't bother showing up on Monday, d'you hear me?

HENO: Is that a promise?

MARTIN: Just make sure you're in here to finish this job, right! There's too much messing going on.

JACK: There's no messing, you just can't work in this cold.

MARTIN: It's not that cold out.

JACK: The only reason you don't feel the cold is because you spend most of your time sitting in your jeep.

MARTIN: Wear some heavy clothes then.

JACK: I'm like Scott of the Antarctic as it is!

HENO: I told him we'd get an electric blanket and wire him up to the extension lead.

MARTIN: Now your tea break isn't till one o' clock. Get back outside!

JACK: Ah Martin, it's twenty to now.

MARTIN: That means there's twenty minutes to go before your break. Now come on…chop chop. Keep them paintbrushes going and you'll keep warm.
(HENO stops working and starts to take off his overalls.)
What do you think you're doing?

HENO: What does it look like?

MARTIN: Get them back on!

HENO: You want me to sign on like this?

MARTIN: At a quarter to one?

HENO: I have to get a bus to Ballyfermot. Or maybe you'd like to get me a taxi or drive me over in your jeep?

MARTIN: You'll have to leave it.

HENO: *(Laughs.)* I will alright!

MARTIN: There's no time to be going off, we're in too much of a hurry. Tell them you're sick or something.

HENO: Tell them I'm sick! Look, if you don't want me signing on the dole take me off it. I'll sign off when I go over...
tell them I've got a job...in the factory?

MARTIN: Ah don't be annoying me!

HENO: I'm running out of stamps, Martin... I'll lose me
benefit.

MARTIN: I'll think about it over the Christmas.
(*Pause. HENO looks at LAR then exits.*)
Just make sure you hurry straight back, d'you hear? (*Walks
over to a pile of cans and counts them.*) How many cans are
upstairs?

LAR: A gallon of blue and a half can of green.

MARTIN: There's a gallon can missing.

LAR: Jack used it for a crap.

MARTIN: Sweet jaysus! (*Sits down.*) I want a word.
(*LAR stops work and sits.*)
This factory, we start Monday.

LAR: Next Monday?

MARTIN: That's why it's important we get this kip finished a
quick as possible.

LAR: No problem...we'll be out of here.

MARTIN: I'm eh, I'm going to need someone to look after it
for me.

LAR: Jack was saying it was fairly big.

MARTIN: It'll need about seven painters.

LAR: I know one or two –

MARTIN: It's alright, I'll get a few kids from FAS or somewhere.

LAR: Will they let you use them?

MARTIN: It's all rough work, iron girders and floors. You
don't think anyone's going to refuse a couple of kids some
work experience in this climate?

LAR: So what do you want with me?

MARTIN: Foreman. I'm giving you the shout.

LAR: But Jack... I thought –

MARTIN: Jack what?

LAR: Isn't he going to be foreman?

MARTIN: You don't think I'd leave him running a job?

LAR: You better let him know. He thinks –

MARTIN: I never said anything to him. So…you'll do it for me?

LAR: Of course I'll do it, but –

MARTIN: I'll look after you, pay you a nice few quid extra.

LAR: What about Heno?

MARTIN: He's a good worker when he's here, but you can't depend on him.

LAR: Oul Jack… You'd better go and tell him straight away.

MARTIN: Not now. (*Gets up.*) I have to dash off and sort out some business. I'll see you when I come back.

(*MARTIN exits. LAR pauses. He looks around then punches the air.*)

LAR: Foreman! Alright Martin! (*He hears the sound of JACK's footsteps. Should he tell him or what?*)

JACK: (*Enters.*) Where's he gone flying off to?

LAR: He said he was in a bit of a hurry.

JACK: He must be up to his eyes, he'll see me later maybe. (*Pause.*)

What did he want with you?

LAR: Wants me to do a bit of wallpapering…a bit of overtime.

JACK: I'll make sure we get a good bit of overtime when we get into that factory. I'll get me son in too. He was only showing off saying that.

LAR: I'd better be getting on with this. (*Tries to get back to work.*)

JACK: I was top man in this firm when his father died.

LAR: Is that right?

JACK: Oul Ned got the contracts and I got the work done… did all the hiring and firing. He ruined it all. Went from painting office blocks and churches to the backs of sheds and rusty fences in the space of six months.

LAR: I left a wall half finished.

JACK: Sit down. We're not in the factory yet. Mind you, it'll all have to change then, you know what I mean?

LAR: Look Jack –

JACK: There'll be new painters there…have to make an impression, let them know who's in charge. Don't worry, I'll see you right.

LAR: Jack –

JACK: Could even finish here by Saturday, but we'll just
stretch it out, make it handy for Sunday. That's how you
get your own back, drag it out a day here a day there.
(*Looks around before speaking.*) He's looking for trouble, that
Heno.

LAR: I have to finish –

JACK: Martin'd sack him in a flash if he heard half the things
he does be saying.

LAR: Once he doesn't involve me with it.

JACK: There's nothing wrong with a fiver an hour overtime.

LAR: Let it in one ear and out the other, Jack.

JACK: If I go off the dole I'll lose the medical card…and me
rent goes up.

LAR: Just look after yourself.

JACK: Thinks all he has to do is mention the union and
Martin'll jump.

LAR: What! Heno been talking about the union?

JACK: They've no say any more, not in little poky basements
like this.

LAR: Maybe this afternoon we'll clean it up ourselves, give
him less to moan about.

JACK: This job is spotless compared to some of the jobs I've
worked on.

LAR: You were saying that Martin was going to clear up what
you owe the union.

JACK: He'll stop a fiver a week out of me wages.

LAR: I haven't paid in years.

JACK: Who has?

LAR: They sent me a letter last month…two hundred and
forty one pounds sixty pence they said I owed! (*Laughs.*)
They want money for when I wasn't even working.

JACK: Ninety I owe. That's a good months gargling gone for
a hop.
(*HENO enters.*)

HENO: It's only one night's drinking for Kavanagh. (*Goes to
JACK.*) Is there any splashes on me face?

LAR: Sure you hardly lifted a brush all morning.

HENO: What did he want with you?

LAR: A bit of wallpapering.

HENO: I'm the slinger on this job.

LAR: It's only a small job, across from where I live.

HENO: (*Sits and gives his shoes a wipe.*) A ghoster and Saturday and Sunday! Who does he think he is?

LAR: It wasn't that long ago you were moaning about no overtime.

HENO: He's lucky I didn't hit him a clatter.

LAR: Sunday's going to be a handy day, isn't it Jack?

JACK: A doddle.

HENO: Why wouldn't any of yous back me up?

LAR: There'll hardly be anything to do.

HENO: If he wants me to work Sunday he's going to have to pay me the proper rate!

LAR: We'll spend all day reading the papers for Christ sake!

HENO: And yous heard me asking him to take me off the dole.

JACK: You'll ruin it for all of us if we have to sign off.

HENO: At least we'll be insured.

JACK: D'you know how much we'll come out with if we work legit?

HENO: He can't afford any hassle if he's about to start a job in a factory. I'll make him get this place sorted out.

LAR: You keep all that talk to yourself!

HENO: I could have a picket outside the door like that! (*Snaps his fingers.*)

LAR: Don't start!

HENO: Are yous with me?

LAR: I'm having none of this!

HENO: Jack…?

LAR: He said he'll be back, come on.

HENO: Telling us what to do now, are you?

LAR: He's mad! Three weeks to Christmas and he wants to start trouble!

HENO: We can't go on like this!

LAR: You're only going to ruin it for yourself.

HENO: Ruin it for you, you mean.

LAR: Tell him Jack.

HENO: Did you ask him if he wanted a few shirts ironed?

LAR: (*Shouts.*) Well I'm having none of it, none of it!

HENO: Jesus relax. I was only getting it up for you. It's oul Jack we'll have to worry about. (*Sings to air of the Red Flag.*) 'The working class, can kiss me arse. I got the foreman's job at last!' There'll be no nine o' clock start with you, what? No knocking off at half four.

JACK: (*Enjoying joke.*) Half eight on the dot every morning!

HENO: You'll look after me and Lar with all the handy jobs, what?

LAR: Were you serious about that Heno…about the union?

HENO: I want what I'm entitled to.

LAR: Who doesn't?

HENO: I never worked for under the rate in me life.

LAR: You have to take what's going.

HENO: You were the same, remember that site in Tallaght, what was it…two, three years ago? (*To JACK.*) Some contractor, a Cork pig, wanted us to work for ten pounds a week less than Malone's men. (*Points to LAR.*) Had the whole site out, chippies, brickies, sparks…the lot! We ended up getting five pound extra.
(*Pause.*)
Men twice your age looked up to you Lar…and now you won't even stand up to the likes of him.

LAR: Another few days, that's all we've left in here. The factory will be sound, you know it will.

HENO: But we'll still be signing on.
(*Pause.*)
Come on Lar…back me up.

LAR: I mind me own business.

HENO: This is your business.

LAR: You'd think there was work everywhere.

HENO: Fair enough, but I'm ringing the union to find out where we stand. (*Gets up.*)

LAR: That's up to you.

JACK: You'll end up without a job.

HENO: So make up your mind which side of the fence you're on! (*He exits.*)
(*Lights fade.*)

Scene 2

A few hours later.

MARTIN enters. He takes out a mobile phone and dials out.

MARTIN: Hello… Is Mr Ryan there?
    (*Pause. Calls.*)
    Lar! (*Goes back to phone.*) Hello Paul, it's Martin Kavanagh, listen that blue is murder to cover, some of the rooms'll need another coat…no, won't cost you more than fifty quid.
    (*Pause.*)
    Of course we'll be finished by the weekend, we're nearly finished the basement now. Yeah…looks lovely.
    (*Pause.*)
    Okay…bye. (*Sees a plastic bag. Picks it up and takes out a child's toy.*)

LAR: (*Enters.*) It's for one of the kids… I didn't want her finding it before Christmas.

MARTIN: (*Puts bag away.*) How are we getting on?

LAR: I've just finished the rooms on the ground floor.

MARTIN: And the hall?

LAR: The skirting's all that's left.

MARTIN: Come on Lar, I'm under pressure, I thought you'd've had them done by now.

LAR: It'll be done by this evening.
    (*Sound of the hall door shutting and footsteps.*)

MARTIN: Who's that?

LAR: Heno.

MARTIN: He's only back now? Jesus Christ, that's it! I'm docking him a half a day's pay! Thinks he can waltz in and out of here when he likes! (*Gives LAR some keys.*) Take some floor boards out of the jeep, get Jack to give you a hand.
    (*LAR exits HENO enters.*) What's your game?

HENO: What have I done now?

MARTIN: It's ten past four.

HENO: I know what time it is.

MARTIN: D'you have to take the day off work to sign on the dole?

HENO: D'you think I've wings on me back? And did you

ever see the length of a dole queue?

MARTIN: You've been drinking!

HENO: I'd no lunch, I went in for a sandwich.

MARTIN: You smell like a brewery.

HENO: I needed to make a few phone calls as well.

MARTIN: Who in the name of jaysus would you be ringing?

HENO: Wouldn't you love to know.

MARTIN: There's no drinking on the job!

HENO: All I did was have one to wash all the dirt from here out of me throat, surely to jaysus I'm allowed that much?

MARTIN: I wouldn't mind if you did some work before you went.

HENO: Isn't the room upstairs finished?

MARTIN: No thanks to you. You'd rather paint over a nail than take it out with a hammer.

HENO: Someone carrying stories?

MARTIN: Just get your gear on and do some work... Finish off the floor boards for Lar.

HENO: You can go and shite! You won't catch me doing any of that work. I'm a fully paid up member me... painter and decorator.

MARTIN: And I'm a brain surgeon. Now if you want work... there it is, if you don't... (*Points to door.*)
(*HENO looks at the door. He walks towards it.*)
Here! Where are you going?

HENO: To work. Any problems sort it out with the Hall.
(*HENO exits.*
LAR enters carrying some wood.)

MARTIN: And how are you fixed with the union?

LAR: I'm not.

MARTIN: You do have a card?

LAR: Haven't paid in for ages.

MARTIN: That's OK. I'll pay the rejoining fee and stop a bit every week. It's a bit brother this, brother that in the factory. Oh and I've sorted out our manpower problems with FAS. Getting four second year apprentices, one boy and three girls.

LAR: Three girls! Aren't you getting any experienced painters?

MARTIN: That's the way it is nowdays, six months with FAS

and you're qualified.

LAR: A lot of that work's tricky.

MARTIN: They'll be alright, you just keep the pressure on them. We've to be finished by the end of February.

LAR: I thought it was March?

MARTIN: Another contractor told Rodgers that he'd do it by the middle of march, I said the end of February and that I'd paper a few rooms in his house for free. Don't worry, there'll be plenty of overtime, you just make sure Heno keeps moving and Jack finishes them railings once and for all.

LAR: I can't start telling them what to do now.

MARTIN: I say what you can and can't do.

JACK: (*Enters with some paint.*) Anything else?

MARTIN: Come on up to the jeep for a second, I want to show you the spess for the factory.

JACK: I'll just take this off.

MARTIN: What?

JACK: (*Takes his coat off.*) I don't want to ruin the jeep.

MARTIN: What's he talking about?

JACK: We're going to look at the specifications for the factory aren't we?

LAR: Martin…

MARTIN: Get that back on and get out and finish them railings!

JACK: You just said –

MARTIN: I was talking to Lar.

JACK: What were you talking to him for?

MARTIN: Lar's going to run if for me.

JACK: Lar…foreman you mean?

MARTIN: No, tea lady!

JACK: But I thought…jaysus Martin!

LAR: I was going to tell you meself Jack.

MARTIN: I don't know where you got the idea from.

JACK: But I'm the longest here…that's the way it works.

MARTIN: Look, I'm not forgetting you Jack. I might have a nice cushy one lined up for you. And Trevor, bring him in in the morning, I'll give him a bit of work for the Christmas. (*Starts to leave.*)

JACK: Hold on Martin! You can't do that...it should be me!

MARTIN: I don't want any more grief. Lar's going to be foreman and that's that! Come on Lar.

(*MARTIN exits.*)

JACK: But I'm after borrying a load of money.

(*Pause.*)

That few bob of a loan was to make up for it all. Thought with the extra pound an hour I could afford it...be able to do the house up and let me and herself finish off our days in a bit of comfort. Now I've gone and let her down again. (*Turns his back to LAR. LAR runs out.*)

She'd her heart set on a new fridge and some carpet...her heart set – (*Sees LAR has gone. Kicks over a can.*) I'm finished, brought it all on meself!

(*HENO enters.*)

Was a hard man, me! Anyone talk to me like that when I was young and that's what they got! (*Makes a fist. Looks out window.*) Now I can't even stand up to a thick like him, me own bloody nephew!

HENO: What ails you?

JACK: Lar...he's after giving it to him.

HENO: He's after giving him what?

JACK: What am I going to do?

HENO: (*Louder.*) He's after giving him what?

JACK: Foreman...for the factory job!

HENO: Lar? Foreman!

JACK: It was mine that job, mine!

HENO: He has another thing coming if he thinks he's going to have the shout over me!

JACK: What am I going to do? I'm after getting a loan of the strength of the rise.

HENO: He'd no right to that job.

JACK: Should've know something like this would happen.

HENO: You're not going to let him away with it, are you? Just once, just this once Jack, stand up to him!

JACK: What match am I?

HENO: I'll back you up!

JACK: It's me own fault for thinking I'd get it.

HENO: If I back you up you'll get the foreman's job.

JACK: It's gone…that bastard has it. He'll make a fortune!

HENO: He will alright!

JACK: He was probably laughing at me this morning when I was talking to him.

HENO: What if you said you were going on strike?

JACK: On strike, me?

HENO: The two of us.

JACK: That man's never given into anyone.

HENO: He'll have no choice.

JACK: And if it doesn't work Heno, he'll sack the two of us. You'll find work but who'll give me a job?

HENO: You can't be sacked for going on strike?

JACK: How can you go on strike if you're on the dole?
(*Pause.*)

HENO: He needs us to finish here so he can start in the factory, doesn't he? Come on Jack stand up to him.

JACK: It's my job by right, isn't it? Do a good job in there and I'll get the respect I'm due.

HENO: That's one thing we're entitled to, respect!

JACK: The other fella…what about him?

HENO: Twenty years with the firm and some blow in is telling you to hurry up, finish that wall, finish your tea.

JACK: He said I've to bring Trevor in in the morning…
I don't want to ruin his chances of a bit of work.

HENO: He only said that to shut you up. You said you were the top man in this firm once…you've a chance to be him again!

JACK: I'm well able to run a job that size.
(*Sound of them returning.*)

HENO: That factory…it's the big one off the Naas road, isn't it?

JACK: Eh, yeah, McCormac's.

HENO: McCormac's, that's the one! Leave this to me.
(*They stand and wait MARTIN's arrival. MARTIN and LAR enter.*)

MARTIN: What's this… Madame Tussaud's?

HENO: I heard the good news.

MARTIN: What do you want now?

HENO: A word in your ear.

MARTIN: You're worse than a parrot, d'you know that?

HENO: Those phone calls…was on to a mate in the union
    earlier today.

MARTIN: And how much do you owe?

HENO: There won't be another brush lifted in here till one
    or two things are sorted out. One, we want double time for
    Sunday –

MARTIN: Go back to work before I lose me sense of humour!

HENO: …back dated for all the overtime we did.

MARTIN: Cop on!

HENO: Two, you get this place sorted out, that toilet fixed!

MARTIN: Anyone from the union come here and I'll tell
    them I never saw you before. You don't exist, d'you under-
    stand? All Johnny Cash, no record of you in me books.

HENO: We've had enough Martin.

MARTIN: Heno, Christmas is that close you can smell it. If
    you don't want to find yourself sitting on your arse for it
    then I suggest you get back to work and don't say another
    word.

JACK: This place is teeming with rats!

MARTIN: Don't you start.

JACK: And there's nowhere to go to the jax.

MARTIN: He put you up to this?

JACK: Are you going to get it fixed or what?

MARTIN: This because Lar's the foreman? You should know
    me better Jack.

JACK: Well…?

HENO: The ball's in your court.

MARTIN: I'm warning you Jack…get back to work now!

HENO: There'll be no threats.

MARTIN: Don't think, for one minute Heno, that I'll back
    down.

HENO: As far as me and Jack are concerned there won't be
    another brush lifted till here's sorted out.

MARTIN: Lar, talk sense to them.

HENO: It's nothing to do with Lar!

LAR: Look there's no point arguing with each other.

HENO: Well...are you with us?

LAR: Heno...before this gets out of hand.

HENO: What are you going to do?

(*Pause.*)

OK, it's your look out.

MARTIN: I'll pretend this hasn't happened, right? I'm going off to organise paint and people for this job and when I get back I want to see wet paint on them walls.

HENO: Sit down Jack. (*Sits.*)

MARTIN: Don't look for trouble with me Heno cause I'll eat you up! And as for you! You'll never work for me or anyone else again.

HENO: It'll take more than that to scare him.

JACK: It was my job, that!

MARTIN: Are you that stupid? It's nothing to do with anyone who I pick for foreman.

JACK: I've taken your crap long enough Martin. I get no thanks, no respect!

MARTIN: You'd be out on the streets if it wasn't for me... who else'd give you a job at your age?

JACK: I'm out on the streets as it is...like a bloody Eskimo! All you can do is laugh and make jokes at me.

MARTIN: Someone has to do the job.

JACK: I should've been someone in this firm.

MARTIN: I keep you working and this is the thanks I get!

JACK: Thanks! You've the neck to talk about thanks!

MARTIN: I've often paid you out of me own pocket when things were bad.

JACK: Me and your father built up a firm from nothing! He'd turn in his grave if he could see what you've made it into.

MARTIN: Okay then...do what yous have to do, doesn't bother me. If you can afford to be out of work for Christmas well and good. But don't come back to me begging for your jobs.

HENO: All we want you to do is what you're supposed to, is that too much to ask?

MARTIN: You think there was work all over the town... think

I just wave a magic wand and everything's grand.

I was given this job on the strength of me price, there was ten, twenty other contractors cut each others prices for this job. I scraped it down to this, if I had refused the job at the price he wanted where would we be now? But

I took it thought it better to take work than refuse it.

HENO: Don't give me that crap!

MARTIN: It's the way things are.

HENO: You spend a fortune every night. And have the cheek to tell me that you don't make a penny!

MARTIN: Of course I make money, but only on the big jobs. That's why I'm in the game. These one's just keep us ticking over, pay the rent.

HENO: It's you taking these skimpy jobs that has us reduced to this!

MARTIN: Alright. (*Throws a set of keys at HENO.*) There's the keys to me jeep. Go out and get it.

(*HENO pauses and looks at the keys.*)

You see it's changed. People are doing the work themselves, an hour in a DIY store and out you come with everything you need to do as good as job as us.

HENO: You can in your arse! There's a skill in this game, you don't walk into a shop and come out a tradesman!

MARTIN: The trade's dead. On it's last legs. Everyone's a painter, they're all ragrolling, paper hanging. What it took you years to pick up is now written on the back of a tin!

HENO: It's not dead, not while I've a brush in me hand.

MARTIN: Look at the stuff you're painting over the damp with. The only skill in that is with the man that invented it…the chemist. All you have to do is lash it on, a monkey could do it, it's the chemicals that do the work.

HENO: Let's see your monkey throw up twenty rolls of wallpaper in a day!

MARTIN: Sure me granny could do that nowdays…it's all ready pasted!

HENO: Look take us off the dole at least, pay us our proper rate.

MARTIN: I can't afford to pay your PRSI. I wouldn't be able to operate if I had to do that.

HENO: It's alright saying that but where'll you be if I'm
    caught?

MARTIN: That's nothing to do with me.

HENO: You'd be in for it if they knew.

MARTIN: You sign on, you work. You take what goes with it
    even if you get caught.

HENO: And you get away scot free?

MARTIN: Now I've a job to organise…a job for you. Lar, get
    the skirting upstairs finished, Jack square the railing off
    outside and Heno…put them floorboards down.

HENO: Shove them up your hole!

MARTIN: If you don't like it you can get lost. I'm getting four
    new painters for Monday so I won't be stuck without you.

HENO: You'll be sorry.

MARTIN: Get to work Logan, while you've still have a job!
    (*MARTIN exits.*)

HENO: A monkey could do it…a monkey! That's all we are
    to him, monkeys!

LAR: Jaysus Heno!

HENO: If he wants to play like that…

LAR: Will you cop on!

HENO: Oh I forgot…you've been promoted you're the zoo
    keeper!

LAR: I only found out this morning.

HENO: You knew Jack was expecting it.

LAR: I was asked.

HENO: Twist you arm, did he?

LAR: Look, this has nothing to do with you!

JACK: What's he paying you…a pound on the hour?

LAR: I need the money too Jack, more than you.

JACK: A couple of hundred if it's done on time?

LAR: He asked me out of the blue.

JACK: You should do well out of him.

LAR: You were never going to be foreman, he told me.

HENO: You'll never have the shout over me!

LAR: I'll look after yous lads, you know I will.

JACK: I should be running this ship Lar…me!

LAR: What could I do?

JACK: You knew I was expecting it, you heard me talking

about it, heard me plans. You should've turned it down, damn you! (*Shouts.*) Should've turned it down!

LAR: But he was never going to ask you.

JACK: If you'd've said no he would've had to.

HENO: Well…are you with us?

LAR: Lads…

HENO: That it then?

LAR: He won't give in.

JACK: Back us up!

LAR: Jaysus Jack… I can't do it…neither can you.

JACK: I can't go on like this.

LAR: If we don't finish here we won't be able to start the factory.

HENO: Now you have it!

LAR: There'll be no work for any of us!

HENO: He was given a choice.

LAR: Choice? What use are choices if you've got no job to go to?

HENO: At least he was given one…we never got any.

LAR: You're just jealous.

HENO: Of you?

LAR: That's what this is all about Jack. He's jealous, thinks there's something wrong with me cause I don't go into the pub with him every night after work. His life's that hollow he has to make everyone else's business his own!

HENO: We're going out. Pick your corner.

LAR: Can you not see what his game is? He doesn't care about you, me or here, all he's worried about is himself.

HENO: You're in no man's land.

LAR: Think of Trevor, he's a chance of a job.

JACK: A few days till the rush is over, a week or two licking Martin's arse in hope that he'll be kept on? That's not a job!

LAR: I'll make sure there's a proper one in the factory for him.

HENO: Just cause you've landed yourself a cushy number you don't want anyone to rock the boat.

LAR: I'm doing no one any harm.

HENO: You're either with us or against us.

LAR: I'm neither!

HENO: It's black and white, no in betweens.

LAR: No, not any more!

HENO: You take the good with the bad.

LAR: Those things don't matter to me any more...almost found out too late.

HENO: Kavanagh can't afford any trouble, there's no way he'd be allowed in the factory.

JACK: He'd be run out of it!

LAR: And if he did give in, he'll be on your back, watching, to see if you're a minute late. Put a foot wrong and you're gone, union or no union.

JACK: Then we keep our feet right...give him nothing to hang us with.

LAR: It's you that'll come out the worst in this, Jack.

JACK: Jaysus man, if we stick together there's not a thing he can do but give in.

LAR: Heno might pick something up, I might. But you...at your age?

JACK: I'm not taking it any more. I shouldn't have to. Just cause I'm old doesn't mean I have to take whatever's being dished out.

LAR: You, above all Jack, know he won't give in.

HENO: For the love of Jaysus come out with us Lar!

LAR: And throw me job away? Leave it there for someone else to pick up?

HENO: In your heart and soul you know we're right!

LAR: It's the same everywhere else for jaysus sake! There's people working in worse conditions for less!

HENO: (*Picks up a crow bar.*) Yeah, in Tai-jaysus-wan! But this boy here won't be one of them!

LAR: You won't be happy till you've pulled everything down around you, will you?

HENO: I'll pull you down if you don't get out of me way. (*Bends down with crow bar.*)

LAR: What are you doing?

HENO: He wants me to work on the floor, doesn't he? Well

I'll work on the floor. (*Starts to rip up the new boards.*) I'll rip
it to fuckin pieces!

LAR: Are you mad! (*Dives at him and takes crow bar.*)

HENO: Give it back!

LAR: (*Pleads.*) Sweet jaysus Heno will you not listen!

HENO: (*Grabs LAR and takes it back.*) Come near me again
and I'll put it fuckin through you!

LAR: Jack, talk sense to him!

JACK: Maybe this is going a bit too far Heno?

HENO: I'm only getting started!

LAR: I'll finish that (*Floor.*) you can start colouring the walls.

HENO: Are you deaf!

LAR: Here, I'll stick on the kettle, get us a few chips.

HENO: Get what you like!

LAR: You're going to ruin it for all of us.

HENO: Ruin it for you, you mean. Ruin your extra pound an
hour!

LAR: This'll be the handiest number any of us'll have in years.

HENO: It'll be even handier when I'm finished with it!

LAR: Jaysus Heno, why are you doing this, we're working,
making money.

HENO: (*Gets up.*) Money, money, money! It's all you ever talk
about. The only difference between you and Kavanagh is
that he has it, but you never will. You'll always have your
overalls on, always crawl from firm to firm.

LAR: Please, leave it out man.

HENO: You should never've left the flats Lar.. it's ruined you!

LAR: (*Starts to lose it.*) If he loses this job!

HENO: He'll be lucky that's all he loses.

LAR: (*Roars at him.*) If I...if I end up out of work over you!

HENO: I'll tear him asunder!

LAR: (*Kicks the bag with child's toy in it.*) Only now! Only now,
you bastard, after over a year of scraping every penny together am I getting back on me feet. Nearly lost me house
till I got the start here and I'm still not out of debt yet. But
if you think that I'm going to crawl back under the rock I
barely crawled out of for another so called principle you've
got another thing coming. If Kavanagh wants shite shov-

elled, I'll do it! If he asks me to jump, I'll say how fuckin high sir, yes sir, no sir, three bags full sir! Cause I've had it with the union and it's lackeys. Now get out of my way before I nail you to the fuckin floor.

(*A pause they look at each other. HENO and JACK exit. LAR lifts up the bag and takes out the broken toy. Lights fade.*)

End of Act One.

ACT TWO

Next morning.

The room is completely empty but for the ladder which stands in the middle of the room and a chair.

MARTIN enters. He calls out for LAR.

LAR enters.

MARTIN: I wouldn't recognise the place…did you do all this?

LAR: I came in early this morning.

> (*Pause.*)

> Look, I tried to ring you last night. There was murder here.

MARTIN: Where are the other two?

LAR: Don't know.

MARTIN: What do you mean you don't know?

> (*Pause.*)

LAR: They said they were going on strike.

MARTIN: What! (*Sees the floorboard split.*) What happened here…who split that?

LAR: Heno ripped them up. You shouldn't've told him to work on the floor.

MARTIN: He'll pay for this!

LAR: We're going to need them back.

MARTIN: That's up to them.

LAR: Jaysus Martin, that's not going to help.

MARTIN: They know where their jobs are.

LAR: They're gonna be out for the day at least!

MARTIN: Drawing the dole and going on strike! In the name of jaysus did you ever hear the likes! They'll be looking for holiday money next!

LAR: Throw them fifty quid each and be done with it.

MARTIN: I won't give them fifty pence!

LAR: They'll think they won and get back to work, we'll have the job squared on time.

MARTIN: We'll get it done if we're to work twenty four hours a day.

LAR: I'm not superman!

MARTIN: I haven't come this far to be beaten by the like of

him.

LAR: Someone has to give way.

MARTIN: They'll soon realise that after an hour or two out in the cold.

LAR: But he's gone to the union!

MARTIN: Union! The union's finished, like everything else. If Heno goes crying to them they'll tell him that if he's any cop on he'll run back to his job before someone else takes it.

LAR: They could mess things up for you, I know enough about them.

MARTIN: Yeah? Well why aren't you out there with them? (*Pause.*)

I'm not going to have someone working for me one minute and then telling me what to do the next.

LAR: You just don't want any bad blood.

MARTIN: Bad blood? I've had so much bad blood I could bottle it and sell it!

LAR: Will you do something before things get out of hand!

MARTIN: I can stick me head out that window and let a shout out: painters wanted, twenty five pounds a day! It'd be like the Pope's mass all over again. Only this time it wouldn't be rosary beads they'd have in their hands, it'd be rollers and scrapers. I could even chisel it down to twenty pounds a day and they'd still some in their droves.

LAR: Then will you go and get someone instead of standing there yapping about it!

MARTIN: All that talk about tradesmen. Shite talk! That's all it is. We're the new frontiersmen. It's not tradesmen we want but rough riders! Anything that doesn't move paint it… Anything that does don't get any splashes on it.

LAR: If we could get Jack in, Heno wouldn't be long following him.

MARTIN: If I know Jack he'll ring in and tell me he's come down with the flu…that he won't be in till next week.

LAR: You give him an awful time Martin.

MARTIN: He's well able for it.

LAR: Then why isn't he here?

MARTIN: (*Pause.*) He knows I don't mean any harm. (*Looks at watch.*) It's half now. I've to be on the other side of town by a quarter to!

LAR: Give it to him if you want.

MARTIN: Give him what?

LAR: I don't care about being foreman.

MARTIN: Course you do, everyone wants to have the shout.

LAR: Will you even need a foreman?

MARTIN: Give me credit, will you!

LAR: Just give everyone a job-lot in the morning and come back at half four and make sure it's done.

MARTIN: That place is so big a couple of skins could lose themselves in it. Got lost in the jaysus place meself. A half an hour I was walking around looking for the way out. (*Pause.*)

Are you sure you couldn't manage here on your own?

LAR: Are you alright in the head? There's a room upstairs to be glossed, six doors, a ceiling that's to be done again, the hall door, the windows –

MARTIN: Alright, alright!

LAR: Could you not stall the factory for a day or two?

MARTIN: Are you joking me?

LAR: We're not going to be finished on time.

MARTIN: Maybe I could get the FAS kids in.

LAR: It's worth a try.

MARTIN: That's what I'll do! (*Sound of footsteps. MARTIN looks up.*)

LAR: It's Jack.

MARTIN: Leave this to me.

(*JACK enters.*)

MARTIN: The dead arose and appeared to many. Did Bridie kick you out of the bed to go out and bring home the bacon?

JACK: She says I'm dead right and she's in two minds whether to ring your mother!

MARTIN: (*Looks at LAR in mock horror.*) Did you not bring Trevor in for the bit of work?

JACK: Where's Heno?

MARTIN: Don't be worrying about him. Just get your overalls

on.

JACK: (*Calls.*) Heno!

LAR: He's probably after getting a start somewhere else.

JACK: Did you stay here all night or something?

LAR: I've the toilets fixed! Told you all they needed was a few kettles of boiling water.

JACK: You two faced bastard! What are you after going and doing on us?

LAR: You can work in here on the walls today. I'll square the railings.

JACK: You can do what you like!

LAR: Come on Jack.

JACK: Was there anyone from the union here?

MARTIN: Yeah.

JACK: What did he say?

MARTIN: I threw him a score and told him I'd meet in him the Shelbourne later for a drink.

JACK: You wait…they'll be here.

LAR: And what'll they see if the come?

JACK: We're still going on strike.

MARTIN: (*Walks behind JACK's back.*) I heard you got yourself a few bob, Jack?

JACK: What are you doing telling him my business?

MARTIN: Seven ton, was it? I could've lent you that if you'd asked me.

JACK: I'll manage.

MARTIN: What's it? Eighty odd quid a week on the dole for you and Bridie? Twenty-five out of that for your loan, same again for grub, thirty quid left! And then there's the rent, the ESB…

JACK: I'm saying nothing till Heno gets here.

MARTIN: You should've took the address of the St Vincent de Paul off that wino when he offered it! (*Laughs at LAR.*)

JACK: (*Glares at LAR for telling him.*) That job was mine!

MARTIN: I say what your job is…me! No one else.

JACK: I helped make this firm what it was, remember that!

MARTIN: Oh I remember what it was alright, Jack.

JACK: Your father looked after his men.

MARTIN: Yeah, when he was sending them down the road.

JACK: He had style.

MARTIN: (*To LAR.*) He'd come in on a Friday and call the men aside. 'How much do I owe you this week?' Then he'd reef out a handful of notes and slap them down!

JACK: Every man's card was stamped. He had the best sign-writers, grainers and slingers working for him.

MARTIN: Oh the best Jack. But what were they slinging? It wasn't wallpaper. (*To LAR.*) Election posters from every lamppost in the city. 'Vote number one!'

JACK: It was worth it for the work.

MARTIN: The job was yours no matter what the price was. There was work everywhere… You could lift up a stone and you'd find a job. The town was being torn apart, office blocks going up over night. D'you remember his joke, do you? The one about the three men pricing for the one job?

JACK: He never shut up telling it.

MARTIN: Tell Lar it.

JACK: Drove us mad with the jaysus thing!

MARTIN: D'you ever hear it Lar? (*LAR nods 'no'.*) Go on Jack…tell him.

JACK: (*Pauses.*) A Cork man, a Cavan man and a Dubliner put in for a job painting the Four Courts.

MARTIN: (*Cuts in.*) The Cork man gives his price: 'Three grand.' 'Break that down for me.', says the fella from the board of works. 'A grand for you, a grand for me and a grand to do the job.' The next one to give his price was the Cavan man. 'Six grand he says.' Two grand for you, two grand for me and two grand to do the job.' The Dublin man was last. 'Well,'…says, he, 'I'll do it for nine grand! Three grand for you, three grand for me –

JACK: (*Steals the punch line. Angry.*) 'And we'll let the Cork fella do the job!'

MARTIN: Politics! That's what made this firm what it was, nods, winks and backhanders. Me father might've painted the inside of many a top man's house for free but he got it back ten times over.

JACK: There's still good work out there but you won't look

for it. Spend most of your time out on the golf links!

MARTIN: I only joined a golf club to make a few contacts.
What happens? I get hooked on the poxy game! I can sink
a put from forty feet...think I can get any work out of it?

JACK: You'd no style, wasn't able to work hard enough, not
like your father.

MARTIN: And look where that got him! Now get your overalls on you while you've still work in you! (*Throws overalls
at him.*)

JACK: (*Kicks them back at him.*) Put them on yourself!

LAR: Jaysus Jack, don't start!

MARTIN: You'll be sorry.

JACK: I'm only sorry I didn't do it long ago!

MARTIN: Five more years Jack, five more years. That's all
you've left.

JACK: I'll pick up something.

MARTIN: Don't cod yourself!

JACK: I'm still a good gilder.

MARTIN: The last time we had a job for that you could get
two pints for a pound! Now I'm going off to get them FAS
kids.

JACK: Your father, God rest his soul! If he could see the way
you're treating me.

MARTIN: My father never gave a curse about you. The only
reason he gave you a job was because you stuck his sister
up the pole!

JACK: That's a lie!

MARTIN: Didn't want her and the child to starve so he gave
you a job. Now I'm not me father. I'll be back with them
FAS kids, don't say I didn't warn you.
(*MARTIN exits.*
Pause.)

JACK: I never stuck her up the pole. Three years married before we had a child. Martin was at the christening...the day
after he made his confo, gave him ten bob for himself.

LAR: You know what Martin's like. He'll be all over you when
he comes back.

JACK: We were like that, me and Ned. (*Crosses his fingers.*) Poor

bastard was only forty eight when he died. We were painting a school, it was tea time and no sign of Ned.

I sent the nipper out looking for him. Found him slumped
across a desk…heart attack.

LAR: Come on and we'll get started. Let Heno look after himself. You're lucky Martin let you in here this morning. Look
around you, the job's oxo.

JACK: It was grand when we left it last night!

LAR: What's the longest you've ever been out, Jack?

JACK: A couple of months maybe.

LAR: Twelve months! That's how long I had to sit on me arse.
Oh I had them all out on strike in Tallaght, got us an extra
fifteen pounds a week, but it cost me, by jaysus did it cost
me!

(*Pause.*)

Should've known they'd be watching me. I came home
from work one night, there was a splash of paint on me
forehead, sky blue. She said it was a lovely shade and was
there any chance of me bringing some home to do the
kitchen.

(*Pause.*)

Union could do nothing, sackable offence robbing paint,
you know yourself. Cause of the strike no firm'd touch me.
And if he thinks I'm going through it all again over a few
mice, a pile of dirt and some oul scaffold he's got another
thing coming!

JACK: We could've done it Lar, if you'd've stood by us.

LAR: No Jack. You're on your own in this game. No one stood
by me when I went for a hop, no one helped me when me
kids were hungry, no one!

JACK: We had him, d'you not realise that? Had him in the
palm of our hands and you had to go and do this.

LAR: I'm not putting me family through that again.

JACK: Now we'll be worse off than ever.

LAR: Nothing's as bad as having no job to go to.

JACK: You wait, you wait and see.

LAR: Did you ever have to crawl, did you? In front of another man? I had to…to me building society manager. The
friendly bank me bollix! Told me they didn't

like repossessing houses, that they liked to give their customers more time to get back on their feet. But a painter? As far as he was concerned I was wasting me time looking for work, that the building trade had collapsed. Told me to cut me losses, get out while

I could and maybe the corpo could fix me up with a gaff. I had to beg that bastard, plead with the pig! In the end he gave me six months...it was like a sentence, six months or they'd take me house back.

(*Pause.*)

I was like a walking chemist I was on so many tablets, me wife left me, thought she was gone for good. She made me a cup of tea one night, it wasn't hot enough

I said. One thing led to another and before I knew it every stick of furniture was in splinters.

(*Pause.*)

There's a dent in the door that I cracked me knuckles off... it stares me straight in the face every morning I go to work.

JACK: It was the way he went about it. I should've been told, not made an eegit out of.

LAR: Sticks and stones Jack...sticks and stones.

(*The door shuts upstairs. Footsteps. LAR braces himself. HENO enters. A pause. He walks around.*)

HENO: Was Kavanagh here?

JACK: You just missed him.

HENO: What did he say?

JACK: Did you talk to the union?

HENO: I hope you're proud of yourself!

LAR: An hour's work, that's all was in it.

JACK: What did they say?

HENO: (*Enters toilet. He flushes it. Returns.*) A proper little bastard, aren't you?

LAR: Look there's no need for this.

JACK: Are they coming?

HENO: What are you doing with them? (*Overalls.*)

JACK: The union, what's the story?

HENO: Put them down!

LAR: You stay as you are Jack, let him mess up his own life.

HENO: (*Grabs LAR.*) Think you're smart, don't you?

LAR: Let go of me.

HENO: Think you're cute!

LAR: Let go of me I said! (*Breaks free. Picks up a hammer.*) Put a finger near me... I'm warning you!

HENO: You haven't got the bottle.

LAR: Try me!

   (*Pause.*)

JACK: Look there's no need for this.

HENO: We could've shown him, me and you. We could've got everything we're entitled to, not just proper money and safe conditions, but other things, respect –

LAR: Respect me –

HENO: Not have to shuffle in a dole queue every week worrying in there's a spot of paint ready to give you away. We could've stopped him making us put down floor boards, piss in paint pots! He takes no prisoners that fella and you want to be on his side?

LAR: Just make up your mind if you're coming or going.

HENO: I'm waiting here!

LAR: What did they say?

HENO: You'd love to know, wouldn't you?

JACK: Are they backing us or what?

LAR: I bet they laughed at you.

HENO: Where's Kavanagh gone?

LAR: Tell him Jack.

JACK: Are the union with us Heno?

LAR: Tell him where Kavanagh's gone to!

   (*Pause.*)

JACK: He said he's gone off to get them FAS kids.

HENO: Let him try!

LAR: We'll have the job finished in no time.

HENO: I'll bottle the first one that picks up a brush!

LAR: A hard man with a bottle, aren't you?

JACK: Heno if he comes back with them kids it's goodnight!

HENO: Threats, that's all it is, threats!

LAR: He's three new painters organised for Monday, there'd be no problem getting them to start early.

HENO: Shut your mouth you little bastard!
(*Pause.*)
You should be ashamed of yourself, turning your back on
your mates!

LAR: Turn me back on me mates! You can talk.

HENO: At least I can hold me head up high.

LAR: Yeah, to throw pints back.

JACK: What's happening Heno!

HENO: You let me down Lar!

LAR: I let you down? I let you down! Jaysus Jack, you can't
depend on this fella... I should know. We were both on the
scratcher then I got this peach of a job to do for a builder
that was starting off.

HENO: There was no money on that job, not a penny!

LAR: We weren't going to make any money out of that one
but we would've made a fortune on the rest of the houses
he was building.

HENO: You'd believe anything you would.

LAR: So I bring Heno along to meet him and what does he do
when he hears he has to graft for a few bob?

HENO: We were going to be ripped off!

LAR: Tells the builder to shove the job up his hole! Wasn't
prepared to graft for the sake of a future!

HENO: No one makes money out of me! I went over to
London.

LAR: After you fucked up my chances!

HENO: Where I was paid for me work!

JACK: Look, what's going on?

LAR: Without any thought for your family.

HENO: They never went short.

LAR: That right?

JACK: For Christ's sake will you answer me!

HENO: Every week boy, every week there was money sent
over!

JACK: Are you listening to me?

LAR: Couldn't even make it over for your yunfella's communion.

HENO: I was working.

LAR: Poor little bastard. He was sure you'd come. Even
waited outside the church gate for you. An hour on a
plane, that's all.

JACK: (*Shouts.*) Heno!

HENO: (*To JACK.*) Didn't I send him over twenty pounds
and a set of them turtle yokes? How many kids got that for
their first communion?

LAR: How could you piss off and leave them all on their own
in them flats for nine months?

HENO: Nothing happened to them, did it?

LAR: I don't know how your mot took you back.

JACK: Look, are we on strike or what?

HENO: I worked hard for my family.

LAR: Worked hard for yourself. For two weeks summer holiday in the pub on the corner with not even a weekend in
Butlins!

HENO: What do you know?

LAR: A day trip to Howth did you, what? A large sliced pan,
and a quarter of ham, a bottle of orange and then off to
Tara St. for the train.

HENO: At least I stood me ground, didn't get too good for
meself and move out!

JACK: What are yous on about?

LAR: I couldn't get away from them flats fast enough.

JACK: Heno, are you listening to me?

LAR: The only reason you're still there is because you think
everyone else's poverty makes you look like a millionaire.

JACK: Will you shut up for a minute!

HENO: Well there's no one hungry in my house. I can feed
them, dress them and still have a pint when ever
I feel like it.

LAR: Five kids in a two bedroomed flat!

HENO: I didn't build the bleedin thing, did I?

JACK: Am I talking to meself?

HENO: (*To JACK.*) It's not as if they're gonna stay there forever. And what's the use of getting a bigger flat and having
it empty when they've all shagged off?

JACK: Ah to hell with this! (*Takes up his overalls.*)

LAR: And you've the neck to talk to me about respect!

HENO: Something you'll never have boy!

JACK: (*To himself.*) Strike! Stupid bleedin idea from the start.

HENO: I can walk into a pub any night of the week and buy a drink for whoever I like.

LAR: You'd rather buy a round of drinks than a bag of coal!

HENO: Well you don't see me bringing home little bundles of wood to heat me gaff! (*Kicks a bundle of wood across at LAR.*)

LAR: No, you'd do without it…like your oulfella!

HENO: My oulfella would've ate Kavanagh for breakfast! You knew him Jack, didn't you?

JACK: What?

HENO: My father…you knew him.

JACK: Look is this supposed to be a strike or a trip down memory jaysus lane!

LAR: Your Da…he wouldn't spend Christmas!

HENO: Jembo Logan! The best painter and decorator in Dublin. Fellas used to come in off the streets to look at his work. He'd be graining a door on the South circular and there'd be an audience around him…you'd swear it was real wood when he finished with it, swear it grew there.

LAR: He couldn't paint his prick with iodine! A pox bottle, that's all he was!

JACK: Like the pair of yous! (*Starts putting his overalls on.*)

HENO: He knew how to spend money, my father. When he went on the piss every man in the Coombe woke up with a hang over!

LAR: Yeah, from listening to him shite talk!

HENO: He had respect boy!

LAR: And he had yous black and blue from all the hidings he gave yous.

HENO: And it's a pity your oulfella didn't do the same to you.

LAR: Your oul wan was drunk for a month after the funeral… everybody in the flats was.

HENO: He made a man out of me, my father.

LAR: A mess of you, that's what he made.

(*Pause.*)

HENO: We're over me and you, we're finished. I don't know

you any more. Larry the scab, that's what they'll call you.

LAR: This isn't a strike.

HENO: You won't get as much as a week's trial as soon as you mention your name.

LAR: Know what the union said to me after I lost me job?

HENO: I'm not interested.

LAR: Sorry was all they said, sorry Lar for all your service, but ta-ta, kiss me arse and goodbye.

JACK: (*Walks past with his overalls on.*)

HENO: Where are you going?

JACK: I've a pain in me arse listening to yous two!

HENO: Take them off!

JACK: Whatever went on between you I want no hand in it!

HENO: I've to wait for a phone call.

JACK: They're not interested in us, they'd've been here by now if they were.

HENO: Listen Jack –

JACK: Piss off Heno, I'm fed up with this, it's a joke!

LAR: Now if you're not going to do any work then get lost!
    (*LAR exits.*)

HENO: (*Calls after him.*) I'll bring that bastard to a stand still!

JACK: Get out of me way.

HENO: I showed them the cheque he gave me for overtime last week. (*Hands him the cheque.*)
    (*JACK looks at the cheque.*)

JACK: So?

HENO: Jack... I know what I'm talking about.

JACK: Look –

HENO: Jesus man, will you just do as I ask?

JACK: That cheque doesn't mean a thing.

HENO: It's proof that he paid me. Now for the last time... get them rags off!

JACK: I've too much to lose.

HENO: You've nothing! Nothing to lose, none of us have, and I'll leave Kavanagh with nothing either!

JACK: She went out and spent half of the jaysus money yesterday!

HENO: Let him shag off and buy all the paint for the factory. That all has to be paid for up front.

JACK: Bought a fridge the size of a tank. A big beige thing, bigger than me. It just stands there, doesn't even make a sound.

HENO: Another five minutes, that's all, another five minutes and I'll know where I stand.

JACK: Lovely yoke for making ice cubes and pouring orange juice out…defrosts itself.

HENO: Trust me Jack! If this works out he'll never set foot in any union job again and neither will Lar!

JACK: Lovely little compartment for freezing bread an' all. And this glass thing for putting vegetables into.

HENO: Look, we'll be back in work in a day, you won't have to worry about the credit bloody union!

JACK: And all that's in the bastard thing is a pint of milk and two poxy eggs!

HENO: Give me patience! (*Looks for some cardboard.*)

JACK: I've to find twenty-five quid a week. All I want to do is to come in, do a bit of work, have me lunch and go home.

HENO: You can't let him treat us the way he does. (*Finds some.*)

JACK: I've seen him deal with blokes like you before. He'd sooner shut down everything than lose the toss of a coin.

HENO: (*Pushes a piece of cardboard into JACK's hand.*) Just take one of these and shut up!

JACK: What do I do with this?

HENO: There's the paint. Write 'strike on here.'

JACK: (*Throws cardboard down.*) Maybe we were a bit quick off the mark yesterday…maybe it was me own fault for expecting to be foreman?

HENO: And does nothing else matter to you?

JACK: Amn't I taking home a week's wages?

HENO: (*Hands him back the cardboard.*) This time next week you'll be on your foreman's rate. An extra pound an hour… Jesus, you'll be loaded man. What'll it be with the overtime…three ton a week? You'll be able to clear that loan up in a month!

JACK: (*Looks for LAR, then at HENO.*) Are you sure you know what you're doing?

HENO: I'm only into first gear, Jack…just wait.

JACK: Bridie says you're right.

HENO: Then maybe you should've sent her in instead of you?

(*Pause.*)

JACK: You better be right. (*Starts to write 'strike on here' on the card.*) Will we have to carry these yokes?

HENO: Just hurry up, will you! I want to be out of here before Kavanagh gets back.

JACK: It's too cold out for that lark. I thought we were just going to sit down...in here.

(*LAR enters. He watches them.*)

LAR: You could be seen by someone from the dole out there.

JACK: We never thought of that Heno!

HENO: What would someone from the labour be doing walking by this kip, at this hour of the morning, in this poxy weather!

LAR: If you're caught you'll have to pay back every penny you collected.

HENO: Let it in one ear and out the other, Jack. He'll soon get worried when he sees we're not budging.

JACK: I don't suppose we can get a drop of tea before we go out?

HENO: In the name of Jaysus!

JACK: What?

HENO: There'll be plenty of time for tea!

JACK: We'll need some heating up.

HENO: Stamp your feet if you get cold. (*Finishes off one of the signs.*) There we go.

JACK: These look stupid.

HENO: They're to stop anyone passing the picket and going inside.

JACK: But –

HENO: But what?

JACK: The kip's empty.

HENO: Exactly, and these are to keep it that way.

LAR: It's not official Heno. I'm not doing anything wrong. I just can't afford to get involved with anyone's battles any more.

HENO: I can! Know why...'cause I've nothing to lose...not like you or Kavanagh.

LAR: Go on then. Get out! Out yous go! But don't come asking me for your jobs back...none of yous!

HENO: (*Mocking.*) The working class can kiss me arse...
    (*MARTIN enters. He has a paper bag with him. He sees the placards.*)

MARTIN: I take it you didn't win the lotto last night.

HENO: Keep going Jack.

MARTIN: Jesus, it's like ice out. Put the kettle on Lar.
    (*MARTIN sits down and takes out some cream cakes from the bag. LAR fills up kettle and plugs it in.*)

HENO: Well?

MARTIN: Well...? (*Eats a cake.*)

HENO: What's the story?

MARTIN: Story? I don't know any stories, do you Lar?

HENO: If that's the way it is...

MARTIN: If you've come in to do some work well and good...if not, keep on going.

HENO: This is your last chance Martin, or this job won't be finished on time.

MARTIN: Oh, them FAS kids will be in in the morning Lar.

LAR: I told you Heno.

MARTIN: Take a cake Lar.
    (*LAR takes one. MARTIN notices JACK staring at them.*)
    Are you hungry Jack? (*Offers him one.*)

JACK: Eh... I'll take one of –

HENO: (*Grabs him back.*) He's only making a fool out of you! Well no more!

MARTIN: You don't think I'm going to eat them all meself... your last chance Jack, before they're all gone.

HENO: If you've anything to say, then say it to me!

MARTIN: (*Glares at JACK.*) Please yourself.

HENO: The union are coming.

MARTIN: Quick, run for the hills!

HENO: They'll soon put the smile on the other side of your face.

MARTIN: Comedians, are they?

HENO: Just don't blame me when you lose the factory job.

MARTIN: I wouldn't lose sleep over you.

HENO: This is official Martin.

MARTIN: Official me neck! I could have the two of yous up to your eyes in trouble.

HENO: It's the employers responsibility to take his workers off the dole.

MARTIN: So?

HENO: I'll report you.

MARTIN: And I'll say that I asked you to sign off but you wouldn't, so I'd no option but to give the job to someone else…as far as I'm concerned I haven't seen you since.

HENO: Never saw me? (*Takes a piece of paper from his pocket.*) And what'll you say about this chicken's neck? (*Points.*) My name…your name.

MARTIN: (*Tries to grab cheque.*) Give me a look at that!

HENO: I wonder does the tax man know about this account?

MARTIN: Gimme the cheque Heno! (*Puts his hand in his pocket.*) Look, how much is it for?

HENO: Come on Jack…

MARTIN: You can't do anything with that!

HENO: Then you've nothing to worry about so.

MARTIN: Is Trevor still looking for a job?

JACK: He's nothing to do with this!

MARTIN: Tell him that when he asks you why he's got none!

JACK: You can't bring him into this…he's done nothing.

HENO: What time is it, Jack?

JACK: Five past ten.

HENO: Have you got twenty pence on you… I've only got a cheque!

JACK: (*Gives him a coin.*) Where are you going?

HENO: He should be in now! Then we'll sort this out once and for all.

(*HENO and JACK are about to leave.*)

LAR: Jesus, will yous not sit down and talk!

HENO: No more talking.

MARTIN: Look what do you want from me?

HENO: (*Takes out a sheet of paper.*) There…our entitlements.

MARTIN: (*Reads from it.*) Tool money…travelling money…

lunch money! (*Throws the sheet away.*) Where would I get
that sort of bread?

HENO: I know how much you're getting for this job.
(*Pause.*)

Five and a half grand.

MARTIN: (*Looks at JACK.*) So?

HENO: Well don't say you've no money.

MARTIN: How long are we here?

HENO: About five weeks.

MARTIN: And how much a week do yous get?

HENO: A ton and a half.

MARTIN: That's four hundred and fifty pounds a week
between three of you, two thousand two hundred and fifty
pounds so far, not including overtime!

HENO: Still a long way from five and a half grand.

MARTIN: And how many rooms had we to paint?

HENO: (*About to count.*) Eh...

MARTIN: Nine rooms, three toilets, a dozen doors, a staircase
the length of O' Connell St and over a dozen sashes!

HENO: So?

MARTIN: Did I get the paint for nothing? Draw it from a tap?
Eleven hundred on paint, wood –

HENO: Look I'm not interested in this!

MARTIN: What about my wages? Have you thought of that?

HENO: And what do you pay yourself...a fortune!

MARTIN: I take home three ton a week.

HENO: Three ton a day!

MARTIN: And that's for petrol, phone calls – never mind pay
the rent and feed meself!

HENO: Would you ever go and –

MARTIN: Do you want a pen and paper to work it out yourself?

HENO: If you price jobs down to the last penny, that's your
look out. It's not going to be me that has to pay for it!

MARTIN: You don't understand it, do you? My hands are
tied, look in the Golden Pages for jaysus sake, count all the
painting contractors! You'd be there for a week, and that's
not including the cowboys.

HENO: Come on Jack, before he pulls out the violins.

MARTIN: If I can't afford to do the jobs at the price people want there's a hundred others waiting to leap at the chance...and what happens to me? I go down, like a ton of bricks!

HENO: You made jobs too expensive, with your...your, jeeps, your mobile phones and your big fat wage packets!

MARTIN: (*Throws the sheet of paper into face.*) There it is boy, in black and white...that's what made it too expensive!

HENO: Don't blame the union.

MARTIN: No one could make money paying out that kind of cash. Jaysus I'd work meself if I thought I'd get that kind of bread.

HENO: No one forces you to takes these jobs.

MARTIN: And no one forces you to work!

HENO: No! Nor never will!

MARTIN: Jaysus Christ man...what more do you want?

HENO: (*Points to sheet of paper.*) It's all in that.

MARTIN: Have I been talking to meself! Were you not listening...the money isn't there!

HENO: Then you better find it.
(*Pause.*)

MARTIN: Alright then...get out! You're sacked!

JACK: Heno!

MARTIN: You get out too, you oul bastard! (*He herds them to the door.*) I'm finished with yous!

HENO: Don't push!

MARTIN: Get off my job now! (*He is about to push them out the door. His phone rings. He answers it.*) Hello? Yeah... What?... Henry Logan? Who's this – (*HENO snatches the phone from him.*)

HENO: About time! Well...did you ring the factory? Game ball. No, he hasn't done a thing, as a matter of fact he was just throwing us out when you rang.
(*Pause.*)
Right...we'll go out now. No, not all of us... (*Looks at LAR.*) Yeah, him. (*Puts the phone down on the ladder.*) Handy yokes them phones.

MARTIN: (*Grabs HENO.*) What's going on! Who are you giving my number out to?

HENO: You'll see Martin, you'll see.

LAR: What did you say about me?

MARTIN: If you mess up this job!

HENO: Come on Jack.

(*HENO exits with JACK.*)

MARTIN: (*Roars after him.*) You won't get me, you bastard!

LAR: What's going on Martin?

MARTIN: Is there another pair of overalls in here?

LAR: Martin, who was on the phone?

MARTIN: I'm not the best painter in the world but I can hold a brush.

LAR: For jaysus sake are you listening to me!

MARTIN: It was the poxy union. That bastard gave them me number!

LAR: What did they say about me?

MARTIN: (*Roars.*) Just give me a tin of paint and a brush will you!

LAR: (*Confused.*) There's no overalls, you'll be destroyed!

MARTIN: Just show me what's to be done!

LAR: The stairs... I suppose, it needs a final coat.

MARTIN: How many has it got?

LAR: One.

MARTIN: How does it look?

LAR: A bit patchy here and there.

MARTIN: Leave it! If it's noticed we'll give it a second coat, the same for everywhere else.

LAR: What about these FAS kids?

MARTIN: Just get going, will you?

LAR: I thought –

MARTIN: I can't have them till Monday!

LAR: What! But we won't make it on our own!

MARTIN: They'll never work for me again! Never!

LAR: What are we going to do now?

MARTIN: I knew Jack was thick! But Heno...he takes the jaysus biscuit!

LAR: I told you he wouldn't back down.

MARTIN: (*Looks out window.*) He's gone!

LAR: Who?

MARTIN: Heno...there's no sign of him.

LAR: Are you sure?

MARTIN: What's he up to now?

LAR: (*Looking out.*) The union, maybe they're here?

MARTIN: All that's out there is Jack. (*Calls out.*) Run off and
left you, has he? Left you to do the dirty work?

LAR: If he's gone and told them that I'm –

MARTIN: Look just get to work, will you!

> (*The phone rings again. MARTIN stares at it. He looks at
> LAR. He answers it.*)
>
> Hello…yes! Oh. Eh…put him on.
>
> (*Pause.*)
>
> Good morning Mr Rodgers.
>
> (*Pause.*)
>
> Oh that? No, it's nothing, nothing at all. Just a little misun-
> derstanding.
>
> (*Pause.*)
>
> Of course, it's all ready over. Just as you rang we were sit-
> ting down to talk it out.
>
> (*Pause.*)
>
> Certainly Mr Rodgers, certainly.
>
> (*Pause.*)
>
> I can guarantee it…just one second. (*Puts hand over phone.
> Changes tone of voice.*) Lar! Get them in!

LAR: What?

MARTIN: I said get them in!

LAR: Who's that now?

MARTIN: (*Growls at him.*) Are you fuckin deaf!

LAR: Martin what's going on?

MARTIN: Get! Them! In!

LAR: Alright, alright!

> (*LAR exits.*)

MARTIN: Sorry about that Mr Rodgers, you were saying?

> (*Pause.*)
>
> Oh the wallpaper for your house? Has your wife picked a
> pattern yet?
>
> (*Pause.*)
>
> And for the staircase?
>
> (*Pause.*)
>
> Right, I'll pick it up and drop it over right away.

(*Pause.*)

I'll send me best slinger over to do it for you next week…
no, not at all. It won't cost you a penny. It's my little way
of thanking you for the contract. (*False laugh.*) Bye… (*Puts
phone down.*)

(*HENO, LAR and JACK enter.*)

HENO: This better be good, I'm after passing me own picket
line!

MARTIN: You're some can of piss!

HENO: If that's all you've called me in for. (*Goes to leave.*)

MARTIN: Do you realise what you nearly done?

(*HENO stops.*)

You could've ruined me!

HENO: (*Takes a cake form the box.*) Stick on the kettle Jack.

(*JACK takes a cake and plugs in the kettle.*)

MARTIN: There's no time for that!

HENO: There's always time for a cuppa. (*Looks in box.*) Ah
Martin, did you not get any doughnuts?

MARTIN: Heno!

HENO: Someone ring?

MARTIN: Just get back to work.

HENO: Nothing's settled yet.

MARTIN: (*Takes out his wallet.*) Give me that cheque, I'll give
you the money for it.

HENO: It's alright.

MARTIN: You won't be able to cash it. The account's empty.

HENO: Then what do you want it for?

MARTIN: Look do you want money or what?

HENO: Among one or two other things.

MARTIN: You know I can't pay you what you want.

HENO: Then we go back out.

(*HENO gets up to leave.*)

MARTIN: I can give you something!

JACK: How much?

MARTIN: What are yous looking for?

HENO: Our proper overtime rate…backdated.

MARTIN: I can't remember all the hours you worked!

HENO: I can…they cost me enough!

MARTIN: I can give you a lump sum…to cover everything.

(*HENO and JACK look at each other.*)

MARTIN: Sixty quid each.

HENO: Come again!

(*Pause.*)

MARTIN: Seventy five then?

HENO: Double that and you'll be close.

MARTIN: Three ton between the two of you? Where'll I get three?

HENO: And you'll be getting off lightly...two fifty each'd be nearer the mark.

MARTIN: Alright. Now can we get back to work or there'll be no money for wages never mind ransoms!

HENO: Didn't I tell you it wouldn't take long?

JACK: That it?

HENO: That's it!

JACK: But what about me?

HENO: We'd better get our gear on.

(*HENO exits.*)

JACK: Hold on Heno! That was part of it. (*Runs after him.*) Heno! Foreman...the foreman's job!

(*JACK exits.*)

MARTIN: If he thinks he's got the better of me...

LAR: What's going on!

MARTIN: He'll earn every penny of it! And if he's so much as a minute late...a second!

LAR: Are you listening to me?

MARTIN: I'll watch every move he makes.

LAR: (*Shouts.*) Martin! Who rang!

MARTIN: Mr Rodgers, the manager in the factory! Someone, guess who, rang the shop steward in the factory...told him there was a strike on here...the shop steward went to Rodgers and wanted to know if it was true that the factory was being painted next week by a gang of scabs.

LAR: How did Heno know who to ring?

MARTIN: What am I, a mind reader? Rodgers chewed the ear off me...told me to sort it out immediately.

LAR: Did he say anything about me?

MARTIN: They were going to back Heno...can you believe

that?

(*HENO and JACK return.*)

JACK: Hold on Heno –

HENO: Look, Jack –

JACK: You said –

MARTIN: What's going on now?

JACK: I'm the longest here Martin!

MARTIN: Jack –

JACK: Twenty years Martin!

MARTIN: I need a younger man.

JACK: But I have the experience, could do it with me eyes closed.

MARTIN: I have a handy little job coming up and it's yours.

HENO: There you go!

JACK: A little shed or something!

MARTIN: A nice cushy one…wallpapering.

HENO: The best slinger on the job, what, Martin.

JACK: It's mine by right!

MARTIN: Look I've enough on me mind right now… I'm still the boss here, still run things!

JACK: Hold on a minute!

HENO: Here, have a cake.

(*JACK knocks the cake to the floor.*)

MARTIN: And you can bring Trevor in in the morning.

HENO: You got him in!

JACK: (*Roars.*) Fuck Trevor! I want this sorted out now! (*Grabs HENO.*) You told me you'd –

HENO: Didn't he say he'd look after you?

MARTIN: That's right…and I'll have your money when I come back. (*Shouts.*) Now can we get some fuckin' work done…please!

JACK: I'll be waiting. (*JACK stares at them.*) And if I don't get what I want I'm going back out there, d'you hear? That job is mine. You know it, Lar knows it…and Heno.
(*Pause.*)
You know it too!

HENO: The main thing is that we got our money…you'll be well able to pay your loan now.

JACK: That job is mine, d'you hear, mine! And no one's go-
    ing to take it away from me!
    (*Exits.*)
LAR: You're some swine, you know that?
    (*HENO laughs.*)
    You could've had us all out of work.
    (*Pause.*)
    You're just lucky, that's all. If we were going into another
    kip like this… You've won nothing!
    (*HENO taps his pocket.*)
    A hundred and fifty quid! How long will that last you? It
    wasn't even an official picket for jaysus sake!
    (*LAR storms out.*)
HENO: (*Calls.*) As far as I'm concerned it was.
MARTIN: (*Returns.*) I don't want any fighting on the job.
HENO: Did that look like a fight to you?
    (*Pause.*)
    Now, one more little thing…that scab goes for a hop.
MARTIN: Go and ask me –
HENO: You can send him where you like but he doesn't set
    foot inside the factory.
MARTIN: Jaysus Christ man –
HENO: He passed a picket!
MARTIN: There was no picket! You were only out five min-
    utes.
HENO: Doesn't matter how long we were out…there was still
    a strike.
MARTIN: Listen to me boy, you don't tell me what to do!
HENO: He passed a picket, you don't do that.
MARTIN: Picket! You and that oul thick a picket!
HENO: He was given the choice to back us up.
MARTIN: And because he stayed on and worked this is
    what's to happen to him?
HENO: He's not setting foot in the factory.
MARTIN: Then none of us will! I'll shut the whole lot down!
HENO: You will alright…you'll go down and sign on the
    dole?
MARTIN: You work for me, remember that.

HENO: It didn't have to be like this.

MARTIN: If you were in my shoes you'd be doing the same.

HENO: You treated us like dirt and made a fortune out of us.

MARTIN: I'd love to know where it is.

HENO: You'd let us sit at home looking out the window waiting for you to pull up in your jeep and tell us to get our gear.

MARTIN: I always called though, didn't I?

HENO: You wouldn't even knock…just beep your horn twice! One morning I asked you to wait five minutes till she came back from the shops…you didn't even wait five seconds.

MARTIN: That's the name of the game…up against the clock, everyone has to duck and dive.

HENO: And now I have you and you're not ducking from this one.

MARTIN: You have me? (*Dials out on his phone.*) Can I have the number for Ballyfermot labour exchange?
(*Pause. Writes a number on his hand then dials it. Pause.*)
Back off Heno…it's ringing.

HENO: You're probably ringing your missis.

MARTIN: (*Hands HENO the phone. He listens.*)

HENO: How do you turn this thing off?

MARTIN: (*Smiles. Takes phone. Thinks he's won.*)

HENO: (*Takes out the cheque.*) You ring the dole office…
I'll ring the tax office.
(*Pause.*)

MARTIN: There won't always be work in factories…won't always be union to hold us hostage.

HENO: Now…you're going to need a new foreman.

MARTIN: Alright… Jack.

HENO: (*Smiles and nods 'no'. He points to himself.*)

MARTIN: (*Pause. Knows he's beaten.*) Will you have me out of here for Monday?

HENO: I'll have you out of here five o' clock tomorrow.
(*LAR returns.*)
I'll leave you to it…boss!
(*HENO exits.*)

MARTIN: (*Pause. Trying to think how to break the news.*) I only kept him on cause he could mullock into the work.

LAR: Well I'll make sure he mullocks into it in the factory. (*Louder so that HENO can hear.*) I'll break his back with work!

MARTIN: Sit down for a sec.

LAR: I'll have the tea room locked too. See how he feels when he can't go for a sly one.

MARTIN: You can sling, can't you?

LAR: Yeah.

MARTIN: There's two rooms I need papered next week.

LAR: Next week? But –

MARTIN: There's about two or three days in it, just take your time and do a good job. It's for Rodgers…it's part of the deal.

LAR: What deal?

MARTIN: I'll pay you the full week.

LAR: What's going on?

MARTIN: I've lots of worked priced, just waiting to get the go ahead, you know what it's like.

LAR: It is on, isn't it, the factory?

MARTIN: What's it coming to when a bunch of strangers can tell you who can and who can't have a job?

LAR: Who can't?

MARTIN: Aren't they supposed to be on the side of the workers?

LAR: Martin, what are you saying to me?

MARTIN: That's what it's all about, isn't it? 'Get the workers working.' But who's in control, us or them?

LAR: No Martin, no!

MARTIN: They've put a gun to me head Lar.

LAR: You're sending me down the road?

MARTIN: Me hands are tied.

LAR: You can't abandon me!

MARTIN: He's made himself foreman, can you credit that?

LAR: I stood by you Martin! You're still the boss!

MARTIN: Boss! What does that mean any more?

LAR: No one can tell you what to do.

MARTIN: That's what I thought. It's me that looks for work…

if I don't get it yous don't exist.

LAR: If you let him away with this you're finished, he'll turn this job into a closed shop, you won't have a say who works for you!

MARTIN: Look –

LAR: Don't take the factory, cancel the lot and let him go ahead. Me and you, we'll scrape along till things pick up.

MARTIN: They won't take the paint back…two grand's worth, Lar.

LAR: They won't stop me from working! I don't care if I've to camp outside the gates in the cold with me kids… I'll shame them into letting me work! They won't stop me from working! (*MARTIN turns away from him.*) Don't let him do it…please Martin! Look, let him have the shout, I don't care about being foreman, I just want me job. (*Grabs him.*) Jesus Martin, I've put me life into me house…tell them I made a mistake…tell them I'm sorry.

(*MARTIN shrugs his shoulders.*)

Me house Martin… I'll lose me house.

MARTIN: (*Walks over to door.*) Two grand Lar…two grand.

LAR: I'll end up on the side of the road.

MARTIN: (*About to leave. Stops. Almost ashamedly.*) Oh, could you take your overalls home and give them a wash for next week?

(*MARTIN exits.*

HENO enters. A cold silence.)

LAR: Why…why do this to me Heno?

HENO: (*Ignoring him.*) Coming into work won't be an ordeal any more…won't have to watch out for floorboards missing, nails sticking up and rats all over the place!

LAR: All I was doing was looking after number one, that's from the same rule book as you.

(*No answer from HENO.*)

Look it's Christmas for jaysus sake! You won, what more do you want?

HENO: (*Pause. Stares at LAR.*) Kavanagh had us down so low, that even the gutter in the street was two feet above us.

LAR: When work dries up, you'll be dumped like everyone

else, where'll your union be then?

HENO: (*Louder.*) We have to stick together, us! Give them an inch and we're gone. We all end up like Jack...and they... they all end up like Kavanagh!

LAR: So we all end up like you?

HENO: Without me brother...it's the end of us all!

(*JACK appears, sullen, at the door.*)

Jack get a move on I want them railings finished by lunch time!

(*HENO exits.*

LAR starts to take his overalls off and gather up his gear.

JACK stares at him.)

JACK: You! You're to blame for this!

LAR: You wouldn't listen, would you?

JACK: I never meant for you to get the knock.

LAR: I told you not to back him up, pleaded with you, begged you...but you wouldn't listen!

JACK: None of this would've happened if you'd've said no.

LAR: You had to rock the boat and let Heno fill you full of crap. Now he's come out trumps and what have you gained?

(*Pause.*)

And I've to do the back hander! (*Half laughs.*) I've to paper two rooms next week so yous can start in the factory!

JACK: If you'd've said no, I'd be the gaffer, we'd've had it so easy...jaysus man, you'd look forward to coming into work.

LAR: At least you've got your job...still be making a shilling.

JACK: The only reason I'm on that job is cause it looks good on a FAS application... 'Thirty years experience.'

(*Pause.*)

Be lucky if that job doesn't kill me. There's walls in there a mile high and a mile long and I'll be the one that has to lash in to them, me that gets the dirty work, me that gets the orders!

(*Pause.*)

There'll be no overtime, not for me anyway. The only thing I'll be able for at five o'clock is me bed. (*Takes up his overalls and walks to door.*)

What have I got to look forward to when all this is over?
Nothing! Five years work left inside me then sit at home
and wait for the grave… Haven't even got the money for
that either.

(*HENO is heard calling.*)

HENO: Jack! The railings!

JACK: Yeah… I'm coming… I'm coming.

(*JACK walks out. LAR is left sitting on a chair.*
The lights fade.)

The End.